Amir Anzur.

INTERNETISM

How to create wealth in the internet economy

@ London
21 Dec 2023

AmirAnzur.com

Dean, WebpreneurAcademy.com
Chief Simplification Officer, aartec.com

"This book is crap. If you are not a billionaire by your early 20s you are a total loser."

MARK ZUCKERBERG

OPEN SOURCE KNOWLEDGE

This book is released as an Open Source book. This means that you can take the content, change the book as you please. Make yourself the co-author, insert your own advertising. Add, delete or modify any of the words.

You can translate the book into your own language. You can sell it (and keep all the profits). You can go through all the words and insert your own affiliate links (explained later in this book) and generate wealth from it.

You can take ideas and words from it and print it in your newspapers or blogs. You can copy it word for word. You can photocopy the contents for your students.

You can change this copyright (or lack of) notice if you wish. You can improve the book and distribute it.

If you find this book or the ideas in it useful than do please share it so others might also benefit from it.

You can give me (Amir Anzur) some credit as an author of the book or ideas but even that is not a requirement.

I made this book free and open source so there were less barriers to helping spread the message about the Internet.

ACKNOWLEDGMENTS

A special thank you to all the "angels" involved in helping to develop this book - parents, brothers, sisters, cousins, investors, colleagues, employees, suppliers, clients, followers, fans, teachers, mentors and friends. There are far too many people to thank and at the risk of leaving people out, I hope you know who you are and I thank you as always for your support.

BOUGHT ONE. GIFTED ONE.

Education and hope are rights that everyone should have. If you donated or bought a copy of this book, I thank you. We have used the donation to print and distribute a copy of this book to an emerging part of the world, as a gift on your behalf.

I hope the person who receives it will appreciate your gift as much as I hope you appreciate this book.

INCOMPLETE CONTENT

There are mistakes in this book. It hasn't been edited by a professional editor yet. I might have repeated myself multiple times. I first wrote the book in 2010 and as of now updating the content in 2018. Not much has changed in terms of the core principles but the world has changed once again due to the smartphone being everywhere. So there might be some minor errors that you spot but it gets the book out faster to you.

The point of this book is to communicate the message of the internet to you rather than a book on perfect writing. I will keep updating the downloadable version of this book and the paperback version might be more stable "releases".

We are using an "agile" approach to releasing this book so as you comment and give us feedback we will go back and improve the book. The number associated with the book i.e. "Internetism-180826" tells you when it was last updated. I.e. 2018, August (08), 26.

To all the teachers of the world.

Whether they be parents, authors, professors, journalists or friends. Those that teach in whichever capacity and format make the world a little better in their own way.

In case you didn't know it, you are also already a teacher. People are following and listening to you. Please do take knowledge from this book and teach those around you about a better world through the Internet.

CONTENTS

1. INTRODUCTION: THE BACKSTORY OF INTERNTISM

"A master has failed more times than a beginner has even tried."

- Amir Anzur

I initially wrote "Internetism" in 2010. I was based in Dubai at the time and wanted to spread my knowledge as far and wide as possible. It is now 2017 and I am updating the book. The principles of Internetism haven't changed in those 7 years. What I wrote still stands. The thing that has changed is smartphones are a lot more spread out so the internet has become an even more engraved part of people's lives than it was 7 years ago. 7 years from today it will only get bigger and even more engrained.

If you are reading this book I probably don't need to convince you that the internet has already impacted the world. I am 40 years old as I write this book. I can remember a life before the internet and smartphones existed. So I don't take for granted what value the internet brings to my life.

If you have ever bought anything online than you are convinced that there is money to be made online as you have spent money online. If you have ever seen an ad online then you know that others are advertising as they know that there is money to be made online.

This book is more aimed at the 40 year old plus market that sort of heard about the internet, knows about doing business in the real world but perhaps might feel left out that they haven't really made money online.

This is aimed at all those ads you see online with young people making it look like making money is so easy and wondered if it was a scam? I can tell you that it is not easy to make money online but if you follow some of these principles it will either save you thousands of dollars in mistakes that I made when making my journey online or save you years of time.

I made my first dollar online in 1999 when I learned about affiliate marketing (marketing other people's products where they pay you a commission). The company was Amazon.com which has now 18 years later become one of the most valuable companies in the world.

2. LESSONS FROM GETTING A HAIRCUT

"Imagination is more powerful than education."

- Amir Anzur

If you go for a haircut in Peshawar, Pakistan it will cost you 100 rupees ($1. Please note: all dollar figures are U.S.). A similar barber in Dubai will cost you 25 dirhams ($7). Get the same haircut in Geneva, Switzerland and it will set you back 40 Swiss francs ($45).

Is Jean-Pierre, the Swiss barber, really 45 times better than Imran, the Pakistani barber? Would Jean-Pierre make your hair look 45 times better than Imran?

I have had haircuts in different parts of the world and can say the results haven't been much different. Swiss barbers don't make you look 45 times better than Pakistani barbers or six times better than Emirati barbers. The experiences are different, but even that depends more on the individual barbershop than on the city. A high-end barbershop in Pakistan offers a similar experience to a high-end barbershop in Switzerland – but at a fraction of the price.

The Swiss barbers are making 45 times more than the Pakistani barbers for the same work and the same time. If anything, the Pakistani barbers have more time for a chat and might even give you a free head massage. Even if we adjust for higher rent, wages and other expenses in Switzerland, the Swiss barbers are making at least 10 times more than the Pakistani barbers while providing the same service.

Now you may ask: "What does a haircut have to do with creating wealth from the Internet?" As you read on, you will discover many of the lessons from the barbershop carry over to the digital age.

Jean-Pierre was protected in the old economy. Imran the barber could not compete for Jean-Pierre's customers. Imran didn't have a Swiss work visa, or the capital to rent a shop in Switzerland. Not many Swiss are going to fly to Pakistan to get their haircut – even if it is 45 times cheaper.

But let's say, instead of haircutting, the job was video editing. Or graphic design. Or software programming. Or customer support. Or math tutoring. Or a number of jobs that didn't exist a few decades ago but are now essential. This change in the economy largely took place just in the last 15 years; the world is only beginning to realize the impact for the next decade.

The (non-barber) Jean-Pierres will face trouble now that their jobs are not location-dependent, while the Imrans will have opportunities. Jean-Pierre can no longer charge his local customers 45 times what Imran charges, unless, of course, he has a trusted brand, strong relationships, a production process unique to his locale or significantly better service. But the Imrans of the world can now get in the game. The Internet means they are no longer restricted by their passport and can serve customers in Switzerland, or anywhere else across the globe, from their home villages. This means their home countries can avoid the brain drain that plagued them in recent history.

Questions of Inequality

One question that might have occurred to you is: "Why are some people rich and others poor?" The average American earns over $45,000 per year, for example, while an average person from the subcontinent earns less than $1,500 per year.

Why does poverty happen? Why is one person a millionaire and another living without running water? Is it genetics? Is it culture? Why are Africans "poor" and suffer from famines? Why is China's economy now booming and what could other countries learn from it? Why is it that one out of every four dollars spent around the world is by an American (US population: 300 million) while the rest of the 6.7 billion share the other 75% of the wealth?

I know you may not expect such deep, difficult questions at the beginning of a book about the Internet, but it's important to understand these ideas before we discuss the modern economy. When you truly understand exactly what wealth is, you will see exactly how big the impact of the Internet is and will continue to be in many societies and industries.

The Internet, like the telephone, the automobile, electricity and TV, is a tool that can help us reach our goals faster. We need to first understand what we want to use these tools for before we can use them effectively.

Peter Drucker, a management guru of the last century, said: "There is nothing so useless as doing efficiently that which should not be done at all." So we need to ensure the Internet adds benefit to our lives before we try to use it.

Or as Friedrich Nietzsche said: "He who has a why can endure any how." The point of this book is to get you to truly understand the "why," because the "why" of the Internet will give you a chance to create substantial wealth wherever you live and whatever your education level or financial background. Not only that, but it can help end global poverty. Once you understand the "why," the "how" becomes much easier to figure out.

If you were to take up golf, the first thing you would do is learn the rules of the game. You would need to know, for instance, that you couldn't throw the ball; you have to use a golf club instead. You need to know that you have to get the ball into the first hole first, and the 18th hole at the end. Once you understand the rules of the game, you can start improving.

If creating wealth is the game you want to play, first you have to understand the game. What exactly is wealth? How can we make more money? Why are some people "poor" while others are "rich?" In summary, how can we create more wealth for ourselves and maybe even help our neighbors to create more wealth?

As an entrepreneur I have spent many years traveling to different parts of the world, where I have witnessed great wealth, but great poverty, too. So the question of inequality has bugged me for a while. And if you start thinking about a problem long enough, you start to come up with solutions.

I have spent tens of thousands of hours figuring out how to create wealth online. I have worked with successful global companies (such as Google, Intel, Microsoft, Oracle and Samsung), governments (such as those in Abu Dhabi, Dubai, Pakistan and

United Kingdom) and international associations (such as the United Nations and World Trade Organization) to understand the bigger picture of wealth creation. I have worked with many millionaires and billionaires, but also spent time with beggars on the streets of Delhi and homeless people in London.

I have started companies in the U.S., the U.K., the U.A.E., and Pakistan. I have been educated in the U.S., the U.K., Belgium, Pakistan, Switzerland and the UAE. The book is meant to give a global perspective on wealth rather than one specific to any country.

I invested time learning how to create wealth, knowing that someday I would go out and teach others. This book is an important part of my teaching. The simple conclusions you read in a few hours took me thousands of hours to figure out. I have distilled the lessons I learned from hundreds of books and many fine teachers, only some of whom I was able to mention.

Whether you are Ethiopian or German, the Internet gives you a chance to create wealth for yourself. But this book isn't about "how to get rich quick." If you're looking for a quick score, buy a raffle ticket and hope for the best. This is more about slowly building riches. The principles discussed in this book will prepare you to win in the Internet economy in the next decade. This could mean finding a life partner, educating your children, creating a living or advancing a cause.

The only way to truly create wealth, though, is to take action. Knowledge, like money, doesn't mean anything in itself; you must use it for something.

The funny thing about humans is that they will do more for others than they will do for themselves. If you tell parents to quit smoking because they are harming themselves, the response might be lukewarm, but if you tell them they are harming their child, they are more likely to listen. Read this book and take action for others; the wealth you create and the lessons you pass on will only appreciate in value.

Is Wealth Possible through the Web?

The founders of Facebook are the youngest self-made billionaires in history. In under a decade, Facebook is valued at a similar level as General Motors and McDonald's, who have hundreds of thousands of employees and took decades to reach the same level of success.

The founders of Google, eBay and Amazon have all also became billionaires in the past decade.

A website you might not have heard of — Diapers.com — sells $500 million worth of diapers through the Web every year. Zappos.com sells over a $1 billion worth of shoes through the Internet every year. Millions of people are being hired through upwork.com and Elance.com. These sites make it possible for businesses in the richer areas of the world (e.g., North America and Europe) to hire people directly from poorer parts (e.g., India, Kenya, Pakistan, Philippines etc.). No visa issues. No minimum wage. Minimal hiring and firing costs. No flight costs. Zero telecommunication costs.

Clickbank.com has paid out over $2 billion in sales commissions for digital information products, yet is probably another website you haven't heard of.

Singer Justin Bieber can thank YouTube for launching his career and becoming a 15-year-old millionaire.

Some internet entrepreneurs share openly online how they make money and teach others, such as Pat Flynn of SmartPassiveIncome.com who makes over $55,000 per month, Steve Chou of MyWifeQuitHerJob.com who made $100,000 in sales from an online store and Andrew Youardian of ecommercefuel who made $1.3 million from his online stores.

I am not based in Silicon Valley, and these words are not aimed at California insiders who invested millions of their own dollars and realized the Web's potential a good decade before the rest of the world. This book is for the rest of the world.

A detailed analysis of France's economy over the past few years found that the Internet destroyed 500,000 jobs. At the same time, though, 1.2 million Web-based jobs were created, which is 2.4 jobs for every one destroyed. The point is, you can see the Internet as a threat or an opportunity. I hope by the end of this book you will see the bright side of the digital economy, which, even if it doesn't benefit you directly, will give your children a better future.

So although a Jean-Pierre could see his job disappear as an Imran can do it much cheaper and/or better, it also allows a Jean-Pierre to now move on to a different job or find a different way to generate wealth for himself. The basic economics of supply and demand are not changing. The Internet can significantly increase supply and demand. The place you were born in or your passport is no longer going to determine the wealth you create for yourself as the Internet enables more people to compete.

A Jean-Pierre might have had a better education than Imran in the past, but this is no longer the case. Anyone with computer access can visit websites such as KhanAcademy.org, Coursera.org, YouTube, Wikipedia, Lynda.com, Google and WebpreneurAcademy.com. There are thousands of niche sites and YouTube videos that teach you anywhere from how to open a barber shop to how to cut better hair.

Before the Industrial Revolution, the normal thing to do was to go into the family business. If your father was a shoemaker, chances are that you would become a shoemaker. With the advent of machine- based production, the more respected thing to do was to work in a large corporation or to be employed by the government.

Smaller, more creative companies will flourish in the next decade, as governments and large corporations begin to cut employees. Larger organizations may make the same revenue, but they won't need as many people. Small is becoming the new big.

Your parents did not make a living through the Web. Chances are they were not entrepreneurs, either. This might make it difficult for you to envision a life working from home making a living off a virtual world.

You are used to seeing people go to work five days a week. Wearing a suit. Going home at 6 p.m. Collecting a paycheck at the end of the month. If your parents stopped going to work, they stopped getting paid.

If you want to become a Webpreneur, you will need to understand how the new economy works. Your parents and teachers might not be the best source of knowledge about Internet careers. Go out into your community and meet a real-life Webpreneur. Go to seminars. Buy courses or books online. Experiment. Only then will you truly believe that starting a business is possible and convince yourself to take further action.

The world is full of skeptics, so chances are if you want to go for something a little unusual, people will laugh at you. Look around and see if those people are living the life you want in the future.

Maybe you are surrounded by people who work in office cubicles all day, every day. Or by people who haven't had much financial success. If you have bigger plans that can help change the world, you might have to break away from these people. The whole industry is so new you need to do your own discovery.

If you are out of school, you need to realize that in the knowledge economy you will be an eternal student. In order to make a living, you will need to continually invest in your learning. The end of studying is not the day you received your certificate.

Even if you are in school, the information in this book is not yet taught in your curriculum. It will open your mind to a set of careers your teachers probably didn't know existed. The Internet gives the learner more power. Rather than having a teacher dictate learning terms, you can choose what you want to study, where you want to study and when you want to study: heck, you can even choose your teacher.

And if you are a teacher, this book will help you cope with the constant change of this era while preparing the next generation to succeed.

3. HOW TO TRAVEL THROUGH TIME

In the movie *Back to the Future*, Marty McFly (Michael J. Fox) is able to travel to the past and the future in a time machine. The ability to travel through time brings many benefits. For instance, the character of Biff takes a current sports book into the past and bets on sports games. He creates a lot of wealth for himself, as he already knows which team will win.

I also learned to travel through time. In 2012 I was sitting in a coffee shop surrounded by cigarette smokers in Abu Dhabi. I asked my Emirati friend what he thought if they ever banned smoking indoors and he said "That will never happen – us Arabs love to smoke too much."

Back in 1999 I was based in Dublin, Ireland. I had asked my Irish friend the same question and he said "That will never happen. Us Irish love smoking too much.". They also thought a ban would never happen in Ireland. The Irish loved smoking as much as the Arabs did. Dublin instituted a smoking ban in 2004. London and Paris followed suit, and in 2010 smoking was banned in Dubai – just up the road from Abu Dhabi.

The smoking ban started in Beverly Hills, California in 1987. If you want to see Abu Dhabi's future, at least when it comes to smoking indoors, you can visit California. And if you are Californian and you want to see what the past was like, visit a restaurant in Abu Dhabi.

Knowing the future is beneficial for entrepreneurs. In the U.K., for instance, the smoking ban meant restaurants could no longer count on fresh cigarette smoke to mask stale carpets or other odors. Dublin- based businesspeople could take advantage of the looming demand for fragrances that would be required in London (and Paris, for that matter). They could, in essence, predict the future.

We can predict the impact of the fast-food industry on many Arab countries. In America, McDonald's, Burger King, Coca-Cola and similar fast-food brands have been popular for decades. As a result, America is one of the most obese countries in the world; over 30% of its population is overweight. As fast-food franchises spread to the rest of the world, we can take steps to ensure our populations do not develop these health problems. We can learn from the future of junk food.

We can also see how other innovations and ideas diffused throughout society. Electricity, the telephone, the printing press, TV, radio and airplanes all spread across the world at different speeds. These innovations impacted each society differently, moving jobs from one industry to another — and making money for those who were prepared for the change.

You might be living in a place where the Internet is not a big part of your life — yet. Just as electricity and mobile phones spread (and continue to spread) across the world, so will the Internet. Perhaps you live in a place where you still book airline tickets through a travel agent. In the U.S., most people book their own airline tickets online.

There are people who benefit from any innovation and others who lose out. You, too, will lose out unless you adapt.

The former presidents of Egypt (Hosni Mubarak) and Tunisia (Zine El Abidine Ben Ali) could have seen the impact of the Internet on politics. In February 2008, John McCain, the American presidential candidate, raised $11 million for his political campaign using traditional fundraising methods. In the same month, Barack Obama went to zero fund-raisers and raised $55 million primarily through the Internet. Obama took advantage of the Web not only to help him raise money, but also to successfully direct his campaign volunteers and followers and ultimately get elected.

Many Arab leaders underestimated the Web's power and were surprised when their people organized and overthrew them. The Internet will continue to have a huge impact on governments, as it gives people a way to connect and organize like never before.

You can take advantage of the Internet no matter where you are, unlike the smoking ban, in which you suffered if it hadn't come to your part of the world yet. If you are based in a developing country such as Sudan and don't have many Internet users in your community, you can still market to foreign consumers. You do not have to emigrate to a major city to derive your income from there.

Ideas don't spread around the globe instantly, and Webpreneurs are taking advantage of this lag, which is called arbitrage. The website Groupon.com, for example, offers its subscribers high discounts in order to get volume sales for its business partners. A $100 treatment at a beauty salon, for example, might sell for $50 on Groupon. The salon would get $25 from the sale, and Groupon would get the other $25. The consumer would save $50. Even though the salon gets only a quarter of the original price, it benefits by attracting more traffic. It can then turn visitors into repeat customers. Groupon is a hit in the U.S. and was at one stage valued at over $6 billion.

Groupon, however, did not quickly enter the Middle East and local entrepreneurs seized the market. Companies such as Cobone.com (UAE), GroupIn.pk (Pakistan) and Deals.Mocality.co.uk (Kenya) used similar business models and took a big chunk of the local market before Groupon arrived a few years later.

Similarly, eBay didn't have the marketing reach for the UAE, so Webpreneurs launched Souq.com to bring a similar business model to this part of the world. These Webpreneurs knew eBay had been successful in America and saw an opportunity to bring the future to their country.

Amazon.com, the largest seller of books in the U.S., sells more books for its electronic reader than it sells paper books. If you are in the paper or printing business, you want to assess how long it might be until "the
future" arrives in your part of the world. Some technologies spread globally within a few years (Facebook, mobile phones), while others can take longer (the car, air travel). Perhaps in your part of the world, at some stage digital books will become more popular than paper books, too.

This book will help you see the future, but the past is also important. You can learn how to "stand on the shoulders of giants," that is, learn from the industry's pioneers. Skeptics in the Middle East, for example, say: "But people here don't trust the Web enough to use their credit cards online." Amazon.com overcame that objection in the 1990s. It is now a multibillion-dollar business. Some solutions will have to be localized. Online credit card use is not as widespread in the Gulf. Emiratis, for example, still like to use couriers such as Aramex and purchase using Cash on Delivery.

But people around the world are not that different from each other. You will see young people using the same mobile phones no matter where they live. This generation has a greater affinity for the world than the older generation. A teenager in Muscat can watch Justin Bieber on YouTube just like a teenager in New York. A few decades ago, pop stars would have been segmented; TV stations in Oman, say, would show only local TV stars.

The biggest musical hit on YouTube ever has been Gangnam Style by PSY a South Korean musician rather than one by an American artist who would have typically dominated in the 1980s and 1990s.

Predicting the future will help you make career choices. If you knew that the TV was coming to your part of the world for instance, you might start a production company, an advertising company or a TV repair shop. You might choose to study mass communication in university.

You have to use your own trial and error to see what trends catch on in your part of the world. Will the Groupon or eBay business models work where you are?

You will find businesses often fail not because of the idea, but because they were not marketed effectively. People laughed when someone came up with the idea to sell bottled water. Now it is as popular in the UAE as it is in the U.S.

The world we live in now allows us to follow what is happening in other parts of the world as if we were actually living there. For instance, someone in Angola can chat with someone in California, watch Californian TV or take an online course from a California university. You might be reading about technology trends in a California newspaper and see, for instance, that Twitter is becoming extremely popular. But when you do your own survey of the Angolan market, you realize Tweeting isn't a big thing. Be careful not to base your business around a trend that hasn't made it to your area yet. You want to learn from the world but be a simple step ahead of your local market.

I can already tell you some good news from the future. Your age, qualifications and nationality won't limit you as much as they did in the past. It used to be that if you didn't have the right degree, you couldn't join the right company and you wouldn't get the right salary. In the Internet economy, you can short-cut your way to a profession instead of having a corporation dictate your career path. You can move at your own pace rather than society dictating your speed. This implies, of course, that it's your responsibility to take control of your education.

Skills such as web design, programming and graphic design are learnable by anyone at any stage. People in their 60s are re-educating themselves to gain the skills to work online.

Being the only kid on the block with a PlayStation begins to get boring pretty quickly. You want your friends to have one, too. It makes gaming more interesting. Owning the only fax machine in the world is useless. The more people who buy a fax machine, the more useful it becomes.

Driving also improved when more people started buying automobiles. The more cars on the road, the better the roads became. More gas stations opened and car companies invested more in research and development and offered more features. Even as things improved, the price of cars came down.

In the same way, if more of us are on the Web, the better it gets for all of us. Governments start making more services available online. More companies offer their products online. Education levels improve faster the more students use the Web to learn. YouTube and Wikipedia get more people to contribute. You can even make the case that the Internet helps reduce poverty and makes the world safer. If our neighbors have something productive to do, they are less likely to steal from you.

You might be the perfect driver, but if everyone else on the road is a bad driver, you still suffer the consequences and get into accidents. This is why you want as many people as possible passing driving tests. If everyone is at a standard level of competence, we all feel safer on the road. We should encourage everyone to achieve a basic level of familiarity with the Web, so we all might benefit.

Moving Up the Innovation Curve

If you have studied marketing, you might have seen the innovation curve. In essence, any innovation usually goes through five stages:

- Innovators
- Early adopters
- Early majority
- Late majority
- Laggards

Innovators buy new products as soon as they come out. They read all the technology magazines and wait in line for the newest gizmo or gadget. Some of these technologies take off while others fail at the early stages. The BetaMax videocassette recorder, for instance, came out in the 1980s, the same time VHS was launched. Many innovators thought BetaMax was superior, but VHS prevailed. A similar competition is going on right now between DVDs, which replaced VCRs, and Blu-ray Discs, which is the newer technology.

In the mid-1990s, innovators started using the Web. By 2015, over three billion of the seven billion people that live in the world were online. Over 1.2 billion people were on Facebook alone. The Internet is now in the late majority stage, especially in the U.S., where over 87% of the population accesses the Web.

In fact if you were to list out popular internet applications as opposed to actual countries the list would look like this:

1. Facebook
2. China
3. India
4. Tencent (Chinese networking site)
5. WhatsApp
6. United States
7. Google+
8. LinkedIn
9. Instagram
10. Twitter

The number of people who actually buy online is a lot lower, though this too depends on where you live. The British, for example, spend the most money online per capita.

Finally, there are the few people — right now less than 1% of the two billion users — who make an income from the Web. But many people indirectly rely on the Web to help them do business. They just don't realize it until their email goes down.

Most people use the Web to:

- Check email (e.g., Hotmail, Yahoo, Gmail)
- Use a social network (e.g., Facebook)
- Search (Google)
- Check their bank account
- Watch videos (e.g., YouTube)
- Read news (e.g., bbc.co.uk, cnn.com)

That is, people are primarily consuming content or helping someone else make money. Fewer people sell their products and services through the Web.

This book will help you, if you take action, to become part of that 1%. Our goal is to encourage people to move to the left side of the innovation curve. If you are among the few who are not using the Internet yet, I encourage you to start, and if you are, I encourage you to become a Webpreneur -someone who uses the internet to make an income.

The statistics on how the Internet is growing around the world are illuminating. Over 42% of the world now has access to the Internet. America has 87% penetration, while Africa lags behind with 26.5% penetration. But the emerging continent has the highest growth rate — 2,500% in the past decade — and the two in 10 Africans who is connected is most likely to have a disposable income.

The penetration of TV, electricity and telephones was also much higher in the U.S. and eventually spread to laggards such as Africa. This book is not a critical look at Africa; as I explained earlier, just because there is an innovation does not mean people should use it. America has one of the highest penetrations of guns in the world; that doesn't mean more guns are good for your country, too.

Mobile phone penetration is still much higher than that of the Internet, especially in the emerging world, and through cell phones, the Internet will spread even faster. Access to the Internet used to be expensive as companies had to dig holes and lay cables in order to connect homes through telephone lines. The cellular networks that connect mobile phones are much cheaper because as the signal is transmitted through the air. The same technology can now be used to provide Internet service to smart phones.

Better roads, railways and communication infrastructure in the past century have helped the U.S. and Europe create a lot of wealth for its citizens. As the world goes digital, emerging countries have a great opportunity to leapfrog others if they invest in high-speed Internet connections. Looking at the growth numbers, it is not hard to convince you that the Internet is here to stay; it's just a matter of whether you will help bring the future to your part of the world, or wait for someone else to do it.

Internet Users As a Percentage of Population

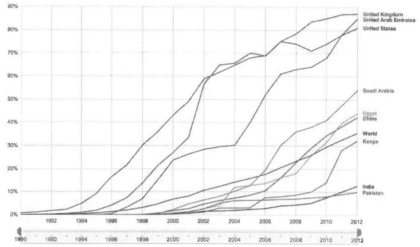

Data from World Bank   Last updated: May 7, 2014

Mobile Cellular Subscriptions (per 100 people)

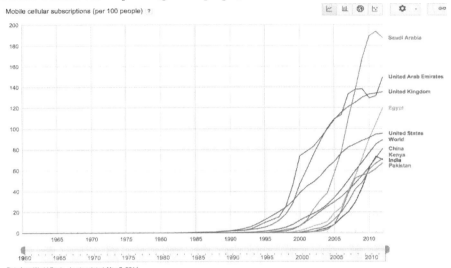

WORLD INTERNET USAGE AND POPULATION STATISTICS
JUNE 30, 2014 - Mid-Year Update

World Regions	Population (2014 Est.)	Internet Users Dec. 31, 2000	Internet Users Latest Data	Penetration (% Population)	Growth 2000-2014	Users % of Table
Africa	1,125,721,038	4,514,400	297,885,898	26.5 %	6,498.6 %	9.8 %
Asia	3,996,408,007	114,304,000	1,386,188,112	34.7 %	1,112.7 %	45.7 %
Europe	825,824,883	105,096,093	582,441,059	70.5 %	454.2 %	19.2 %
Middle East	231,588,580	3,284,800	111,809,510	48.3 %	3,303.8 %	3.7 %
North America	353,860,227	108,096,800	310,322,257	87.7 %	187.1 %	10.2 %
Latin America / Caribbean	612,279,181	18,068,919	320,312,562	52.3 %	1,672.7 %	10.5 %
Oceania / Australia	36,724,649	7,620,480	26,789,942	72.9 %	251.6 %	0.9 %
WORLD TOTAL	7,182,406,565	360,985,492	3,035,749,340	42.3 %	741.0 %	100.0 %

Source: InternetWorldStats.com

4. A BRIEF HISTORY OF MONEY

Most people want to be rich, but what exactly is money? In this chapter we will go back to the basics of wealth creation. Remember, in order to win any game, you need to understand the rules. If the game you want to play is Who Has the Highest Number in his or her Bank Account, you should understand how to achieve that number .

Let's assume that wealth means how much money you have. The more money you have, the richer you are. I know money does not buy you happiness, but I am sure you would rather be rich and unhappy than poor and unhappy.

From the Gift to the Virtual Economy

A few thousand years ago, humans lived in a gift economy. We lived in small communities and would not expect anything in return if we performed a task or gave something to someone. If you caught a fish, you
would give it to your friend without expecting anything in return. This is similar to what you might still have with your immediate family; if you make your brother a meal, you do not expect him to make one in return.

As communities began to grow, more people became strangers, who were less trusted. The gift economy gave way to **bartering**. Now if you had spare fish, you could exchange them for a farmer's spare carrots.

Eventually this, too, became a hassle. If you had spare fish and needed shoes but the shoemaker didn't need fish, you would have to find a third party who had something the shoemaker needed. Complicated, right? That's why **commodity money** was introduced.

Now you could trade your fish for coins, which you could then spend on whatever you wanted. When you went to buy shoes, you would hand the shoemaker a gold coin, which he could then spend on whatever he wanted. Commodity money was usually gold, silver, copper or even barley; that is, it had value in and of itself.

If you imagine a large trade overseas, you can probably see the problem with commodity money. Who wants to haul a shipful of gold across the water? This led to the idea of **representative money**.

Representative money is the currency you are used to: the dollar, the euro, the rupee, the dirham, etc. The actual coins or banknotes are not really worth what they represent. A $100 bill is not worth $100. We as society have agreed that the note that says "$100" can be used to buy other products and services that represent $100.

In the past few decades, we have even moved on to **virtual money**. Now if you want to buy something you give the shop your credit card, which tells your bank to subtract a number from your bank account and add a number to the seller's bank account. When you do an online bank transfer the same thing happens. Numbers are exchanged in databases but nothing physical moves.

You can say you are a millionaire, but it's just a number in a database. Wealth is important, but too often we let a number cause us stress. It works the other way, too. If you feel financially strapped, remember, all you have to do is to figure out how to make that number positive and as large as possible. At the end of the day, the number still represents **value**; the more fish you can catch and sell, the higher the number.

5. THE SIMPLE WEALTH FORMULA

Now that we understand how the scoring works, let us simplify the formula for creating wealth:

	Amount of Value You Can Add
X	Number of People You Can Impact
–	Number of People Who Can Do What You Do
–	Cost to Serve
=	Total Wealth Created

If you understand basic algebra, you see you want to make the top two parts of the equation as big as possible and the bottom two as low as possible. Let's look at each of the factors and see how the Internet helps you manipulate the equation.

A little disclaimer about the formula – this is meant to help you understand the bigger picture of how you can create wealth rather than a "plug and play" of numbers. Look at increasing or decreasing the factors and how it will impact your business or personal wealth rather than looking for exact values to put in.

AMOUNT OF VALUE YOU CAN ADD

You might tip a doorman $1 since he saved you the effort and time by opening the door for you. If you needed a heart surgeon, you would give him $10,000 (and probably whatever you had) since he could save your life.

The value provided by the heart surgeon is much greater than the value provided by the doorman, which is why a heart surgeon makes a lot more money than a doorman.

There is one thing that you and Bill Gates have in common. We all have the same amount of time: 24 hours a day. But the more value you can create for each of those hours, the more wealth you will create.

The CEO of a large corporation makes over a hundred times what an average employee makes, because if the CEO helps 1,000 employees generate an extra $100 per year, the corporation makes an extra $100,000 per year. If a manager lower in the company helps all 10 of his employees make an extra $100, the company makes only $1,000 more. The value the CEO provides is much greater than that of the manager, so the CEO is compensated more.

Let's look at an example of a $20 book sold by Amazon.com. Value is created and money paid to different people in the chain:

- $20 is taken from your bank account and added to a retailer such as Amazon.com.
- $1 is given to Visa for processing the credit card transaction
- $4 is given to DHL for delivering the book
- $2 is given to the printers
- $7 is given to the publisher for marketing and distributing
- $2 is given to the author for writing the book
- $2 is given to the affiliate that helped bring the sale to Amazon
- $2 is kept as profit for Amazon

Multiple parties make money of this one transaction. Nothing material is exchanged – databases communicate with each other and transfer the appropriate amount to everyone who has provided value to you.

To make money, you have to figure out a way to **provide value to the world**. The more value you can provide, the more money you will make. I am using Microsoft Office to write this book. I paid $100 to buy a copy but feel I am getting more than $100 worth of value and so I am happy to have paid that price.

If you paid $20 for this book, you should get at least $20 worth of entertainment or education to feel good about the transaction. If you think you got fair value for this book, you are more likely to recommend it to a friend or buy my next book. If you think you overpaid, I am not likely to grow my businesses.

As long as you can give a greater amount of value than you charge you will create wealth for yourself.

Using Shovels or Teaspoons

If you are asked to dig a giant hole in the ground, would you use a teaspoon or a shovel?

The answer depends on how you are getting paid. If you are making a high hourly wage then you might as well use the teaspoon; the longer you can make the task last, the more money you make. It doesn't matter how fast you dig.

If you are an entrepreneur, chances are you are getting paid by the number of holes you dig. You want to dig as quickly as possible, so you would use a shovel rather than a teaspoon; if you could find digging equipment to do the job even faster, you would use that instead.

Remember, in most cases the world rewards you for the **value you create**, not the time you spent to create that value. For instance, do you care if this book took me a week to write or a few years to write? The output is what you are concerned with; if I could have created the same-quality book in half the time, I would have doubled my return on investment.

It is the same for most creative work. You care about the emotional impact of the movie, the quality of the song or the user-friendliness of the software, not how long it took to create.

Education can increase potential value. If you didn't know shovels existed, you would have no choice but to use a teaspoon. If someone demonstrated a shovel, you would realize the tool's dramatic effect on your hole-digging time and use it right away. You would also quickly adopt a more efficient shoveling technique if it were taught to you.

We used to have to write letters with a pen and paper. If you had a business idea and wanted to tell 10 people about it, you would need 10 hours to do the writing. If half the people who read your letter gave you $100, you would end up with $500 or $50 per hour. With word- processing software such as Microsoft Word it might still take you an hour to produce the first letter but less than a minute to print out the other nine copies. You would still make $500 but for only one hour's work. Technology and education in this example have enabled you to increase your hourly rate to $500 an hour.

It sounds basic, but this is how the wealth of nations has been created. An American farmer has agricultural machinery that allows him to do the equivalent work of a hundred farmers based in Bangladesh. The American farmer's hourly output is significantly higher.

Education in developed countries has been traditionally much better than in developing countries, so their citizens have been able to produce more per hour.

Imagine a farmer in an emerging part of the world who needs to sell his vegetables. If he doesn't have a car, it might take him two days to get his produce to market. A developed-country farmer would have a truck that would enable him to make the same journey in an hour. The value a developed-country farmer gives to the world is higher because of his superior equipment. Of course, fancy tools would be useless if the farmer didn't know how to use them. Many people have access to the Internet, but they do not know how to use it to save time or create wealth.

While passing a construction site in Pakistan I suddenly could see why some countries are developing countries while others are considered developed. A bricklayer was standing on a pile of bricks that he needed to pass on to the first floor of the construction site. I watched for about 20 minutes on how he would pick up one brick and throw it up. Brick by brick they went through this process. In the developed economy the same process would take one person with a fork lift. What would take two people 8 hours to complete in the developing world a more educated and having access to better tools would require a single fork lift driver in 15 minutes.

Remember that the outcome of getting the bricks to the first floor is what is required rather than how long it takes for the task. In developed world economies there are better tools available.

If you compare the efficiency of motion of a human compared to the other animals we come a long way down the list where there are much more efficient animals such as the vulture which can be much more efficient than us. But when you compare a human with their tools such as a bicycle or a car than humans beat all other animals. It is that access to the tools and the knowledge to use the tools that is important.

With the internet the tool is the computer and this computer can be in the form of a smart phone or laptop. Smart internet entrepreneurs know how they can leverage their relationships online. You might for instance have entered your name and email address on a website. Soon you start receiving emails which begin with your name. As you might be aware the internet entrepreneur isn't sitting down and writing individual emails to all her customers but instead uses email automation software like MailChimp or aweber to automate the relationship building process with thousands of people that might be virtually impossible in the offline world.

I have thousands of subscribers to my blog at www.AmirAnzur.com. In the grand scheme of things a few thousand subscribers is miniscule. But every time I write a new blog post it is like having a conversation with over 2,000 people. It doesn't take me any extra work if there are 2,000 or 10 people on the list. But this tool of a blog is using a shovel to build my relationships online.

Figure 1 - A Pakistani brick layer passing up one brick at a time to his colleague.

Perceived Value

Perceived value is also important in wealth creation. You might notice that when you buy original software, the physical disc comes in a big package. This makes consumers think they are getting more. Consumers are just beginning to appreciate the value of digital products.

When you fly first-class on an airline, the airline gives you nice cutlery, dishes and better food to increase the perceived value of your experience and justify the cost, which is double or triple that of an economy ticket.

If you go to a high-end barbershop, it might offer you tea or coffee. The cost of the tea is minimal, but it improves the experience and justifies the higher price.

This perceived value is also where the importance of country branding comes in. After I started Webpreneur Academy I briefly moved to Pakistan as I wanted to teach there. But my sales got impacted – the perceived value of a British educational brand is much higher than the perceived value of a Pakistani educational brand – even though I am the same person. I've learnt to leverage my Britishness for selling online. The perceived value is why your government needs to help its citizens be perceived as a higher value – especially in the services economy where more and more of the output is virtual rather than physical.

Impact of the Web on Value Creation

The Internet impacts your ability to create more value and hence more wealth. In the old economy, I as an author would need to find a publisher. For editing, printing and marketing a book, a publisher would receive approximately $7 of the $20 price. If the book were sold through a traditional store in a shopping mall, a retailer would keep $7 to cover its costs (e.g., rent, salaries). In the end, I would take home only $2.

Now I can publish directly through websites such as Lulu.com and CreateSpace.com. Once I have written the book, I simply upload it and choose the Print On Demand service. When you order the book through Amazon, for example, Lulu or CreateSpace prints a single copy and ships it to you.

This drastically changes the book publishing industry. I can do the marketing and promotion myself, then direct my customers to order from a website, which then fills the orders. Instead of making $2, I can now take home at least $9 of the $20. In return for the bigger percentage, though, I had to create more value than the traditional publisher model. As we create more value, we make more money. This is how Nick Stephenson has managed to build up a business earning well over a $150,000 per year selling books directly to his readers of his fiction books. He is probably a name you never heard of yet is an example of thousands of authors making a living through carving a niche for themselves without the traditional publisher.

Let's say you were a journalist before the Web came along. You made a salary (usually relatively low) in exchange for the articles you wrote.

The articles appeared in a newspaper, which made money by selling advertising to accompany the articles.

In the Internet economy, you can start a blog or website and publish the same article. Instead of having an editor vet your stories or a salesperson sell advertising space, you can control more of the value chain. You can start your own free website at sites such as WordPress.com(visit www.amiranzur.wordpress.com to see an example), Tumblr.com or Blogger.com. You can now publish your article for free. You do not need to pay for an expensive printing press, a distributor to get your articles on newsstands or an advertising salesperson.

You can then sign up for an affiliate account with Amazon.com, which will give you 5-15% commission for any products you help it sell. This is an automatic deal that everyone can sign up for; you do not need an agent to convince Amazon.

If 1,000 people come to your website and read an article, perhaps 100 will click on Amazon's banner, let's say an ad for a $10 book. Of those 100, maybe 10 end up buying the book. Amazon gives you 10%, or $1 for every book it sells, which means you would make $10 for every 1,000 visitors.

The nice thing about this is you don't have to do any more work whether 100 people visit your website or a million, whether 10 books are sold or 1,000. Just the amount you make increases.

A second method to make money from your article is to sign up with Google AdSense. This is also free. Google will use a little bit of your website real estate to show ads, which it finds for you. The search engine has an automated program that determines what ads are most relevant to your content and therefore most likely to be clicked. If your website were about pets, it would display dog food ads, for example. If someone clicks on the ad to go through to an advertised website, Google charges that advertiser $1, half of which it gives to you. Depending on your content, you can make a lot more than $1 per click. Advertisers for certain types of insurance and financial-based products, for instance, pay more. In effect Google is like a real estate agent in renting out your real estate space to advertisers and taking a commission.

In this scenario, you took care of advertising sales (with Amazon or Google AdSense, both of which required minimal set-up and cost nothing), printing (your free Wordpress/Tumbr/Blogger website; you can also buy your own domain by visiting HostMarkaz.com or HostGator.com) and distribution (people get your content on their home computers rather than having to go to a newsstand).

You can now make money directly rather than getting a job at a newspaper. Of course, this is not as easy as I make it seem; your articles have to be popular and your readership takes time to grow. But, if you have the perseverance, you can be successful.

Arianna Huffington who founded TheHuffingtonPost.com used this model and was eventually bought out by AOL Time Warner for $315 million. Newspaper publishing is a good example of how the Internet destroyed millions of jobs (sales executives, distributors, printers) but created millions more (journalists, writers, content creators).

If you live in Ethiopia, for instance, you can publish your online newspaper and target Ethiopians living in the U.S. Even if you get just 1,000 readers from each state, you would have 50,000 customers. In the old economy this would be difficult as the cost of distributing only 1,000 newspapers would be too high. If you couldn't sell the papers, you lost money. Unencumbered by printing or distribution costs, you can quickly change your online focus, from the U.S. market to London or Tokyo, for example.

You can see how you can add a lot more value to the world via the Web. The process of printing, sales and distribution has been automated, giving you more power. All you need to focus on now is creating better content.

In many countries you needed a license to become a journalist; on the Internet you already have permission to write. You used to need a publisher to tell you your book was worth publishing; on the Internet you can post whatever you like. The only thing stopping you is your mindset and time — there are only 24 hours in a day, even for Bill Gates.

NUMBER OF PEOPLE YOU CAN IMPACT

If our heart surgeon made $1,000 per operation and could treat 10 people a day, he would make $10,000. If he could help 100 people, he would make $100,000.

Bill Gates became one of the richest people in the world because his software was able to impact millions of people. The world's richest entertainer, Oprah Winfrey, had a TV show that was watched by millions.

An actor living in an African village might make a few thousand dollars in plays at the local theater. Tom Cruise might make $20 million per movie that play in cinemas around the world. Millions pay. The African actor and Tom Cruise both have to learn their lines, put in the same effort and do the same work. But Tom Cruise impacts millions and hence creates a lot more wealth.

For thousands of years, restaurateurs usually owned one or two establishments, usually in their neighborhood, where they keep an eye on them. The late Ray Kroc, who founded McDonald's, became one of the richest men in the world because he came up with systems and processes that enabled anyone in the world to run one of his restaurants. There are now over 33,000 McDonald's that employ 400,000 employees worldwide. Owning a system that facilitated over 100 billion hamburgers to be served is more lucrative than owning a small restaurant serving a few hundred local customers.

McDonald's does not own all its restaurants, but its system allows entrepreneurs to run their own restaurants using the company's brand and formula for success. Kroc made his fortune by finding a way to impact more people.

Again, I am typing this document using Microsoft Word. Microsoft spent millions to create the first version of its word-processing software. But each successive copy costs next to nothing, requiring just a click of a computer button. Yet Gates' company makes $100 for each copy of Word. Imagine how many millions of people around the world use this software. Multiply that number by $100. That's why Bill Gates is one of the richest people in the world.

One reason an average American makes $45,000 per year while an average Pakistani makes $1,500 is that American companies impact more people. America has free trade with its neighbors Canada and Mexico. Pakistan has limited trade with India, even though deregulating would give it access to a billion more customers. Most of the 300 million Americans speak the same language, English. Multiple languages are spoken in Pakistan. America's roads, railways, airports and harbors make it easier to reach more people, quicker. Pakistan's transportation infrastructure is not as sophisticated especially to remote villages.

Americans can also travel easier, making it easier to spread their ideas and products across the globe. There might be a Pakistani Bill Gates, but he is probably stuck in a line, waiting for a travel visa.

Impact of the Web on Number of People Impacted

How can the Internet help you impact more people? Imagine you were a journalist in Johannesburg before the Web caught on. The only people who could read your articles were South Africans, and even they had to pick up the newspaper on the day your article was published. If they were out of town or too busy to read the paper that day, you got one less reader.

Now, as soon as your article is posted on the Internet, people can read it, and not just in Johannesburg. Your potential readership includes anyone with Web access, three billion rather than a few million. People don't have to read your article on the day it is published, either; they can read it any time, even in a few years, and anywhere, even on vacation. The work you did to write the article is the same, but now you have an asset that can bring in money (through online advertising) for years.

Imagine you ran a great bakery in the old economy. You would rely on word-of-mouth; that is, customers recommending your bakery to their friends. Before mobile phones and Facebook, people would keep in touch with fewer people. Now, an average Facebook user has 130 friends. If someone has a great experience in your bakery, he or she spreads the word online to hundreds or thousands of potential customers.

In the old economy, it was difficult to get a food critic to write about your bakery. A review in a newspaper or magazine would attract more customers, but the number of journalists was limited. Now you can approach one of the thousands of food bloggers to write about your bakery. The exposure should lead to more cake sales.

A local bookstore's customers are limited to those within driving distance. An online store such as Amazon can start a website and instantly start serving the millions of book lovers around the world.

There are only so many feet in a neighborhood, which used to limit a shoemaker's clientele. Plus, not everyone wanted the same shoes, so the shoemaker had to produce different styles. Companies such as Nike and Adidas made millions for their founders because they were able to make distribution deals to sell their shoes through retailers around the world. Now an entrepreneur such as Blake Mycoskie can launch www.toms.com and sell over 600,000 pairs of shoes.

It used to be that if you enjoyed a book and wanted to recommend it to your parents, you had to write a letter, buy a stamp and post it. A few days later, they would get your letter and maybe buy the book. Now you can email a hundred people at once, hit "like" on Facebook, or create a short video review, upload it to YouTube and tell the world about the book (this one, I hope). And those people in turn can email another hundred people or hit "like" on Facebook or spread the word in different ways. This is known as the viral effect. A large amount of wealth has been created by the viral effect.

The Internet gives you leverage, the ability to impact more with less. If you spend days working on a great presentation, you can now record it with a video camera and post it online. You still use PowerPoint and deliver the presentation to an audience, but with only one extra visitor, the video camera, you can reach people across the world. They can benefit from your presentation today, tomorrow or next year and you don't have to do any extra work. If you are not already doing it think of every presentation you have to give as a chance to build up your digital asset – record it and post it online.

What if you could hire one more salesperson? And what if that salesperson could work all day, all year? That is what the Internet does for your business; 24 hours a day, seven days a week, it sells your product and services to anyone, anywhere.

The Internet opens up trade for closed countries. Indians can hire Pakistanis online, and Pakistanis can collaborate with Indians; the governments haven't blocked IP addresses across borders — yet! Instead of lining up for a visa, the Pakistani Bill Gates can spend his time exposing his products to the world. Even the trade embargoes imposed on Iranians are easier to circumnavigate through the Internet.

The Internet breaks down political barriers and simply lets entrepreneurs create wealth as governments can't interfere with ecommerce as they do with the rest of the economy. More trade with more people leads to greater wealth for the world.

NUMBER OF PEOPLE WHO CAN DO WHAT YOU DO

It is relatively easy to become a doorman. You can learn the job in less than an hour. To become a good heart surgeon, you need to spend years at medical school. Any heart surgeon can become a doorman, but not every doorman can become a heart surgeon.

Since heart surgeons are more rare, they can charge more for their time. Superstar singers such as Celine Dion charge over a million dollars to perform at a private party. Why? Because there is only one Celine Dion. You can play her CDs. You can even hire a Celine Dion look-alike to sing at your party, but you will not pay her nearly as much as the real Celine Dion.

This part of the formula also explains why protecting intellectual property is important for creating wealth. In the U.S., intellectual property rights are relatively strong, so when an artist records a CD, it is illegal to copy it. The singer and the record company earn revenue with every CD sold. In the emerging world, intellectual property protection is weaker. Cassette tapes, CDs and digital copies of an artist's songs are available everywhere for free. The artists do not generate any money from CD sales, so there is little incentive for them to promote their music or grow their careers. If they can't make enough money through live performances, they might have to get a regular job.

Nike doesn't sponsor many sports stars in emerging countries, because there are so many Nike knock-offs on the market. Nike doesn't profit from advertising in countries with weak intellectual property rights, and without Nike's sponsorship, athletes do not have the money to play the sports they love for a living.

In the U.S. and the U.K. over 300,000 books are published annually. Authors know they can make an income through their book sales. In many emerging countries, books are simply photocopied without recourse from the government. There is no incentive for publishers to spend time and money marketing books that can be copied for free. In developed economies you can go to jail for photocopying books without the author's permission. Authors become unique and thus can generate more wealth. Before the internet came along many books were simply not available in the developing economies – now especially as more books go digital everyone has access to the same knowledge.

Begin Youism

There are two types of goods: commodities and brands. Gold, silver, copper and steel are examples of commodities. You don't pay much attention to brand, because the gold from one seller is the same as the other. You buy from whomever is the cheapest.

It's harder to calculate the price for a brand. Someone might pour you a drink that tastes exactly the same as Coca-Cola, but if you know it isn't the real thing, you probably won't enjoy it as much. That is why Coca-Cola's brand is worth billions of dollars. Shoes made of exactly the same quality materials but without the Nike "Swoosh" logo will sell for a lot less than branded Nikes.

Humans can also be commodities and brands. If you are a commodity, you will make a relatively low salary. You cannot be differentiated. For instance, if you work in a McDonald's, your salary will be relatively low as there are millions of other people who can do your job. McDonald's training process has made it so that most people can learn it.

On the other hand, Pablo Picasso's paintings sell for millions of dollars. Someone else could paint the same painting, using similar materials and techniques, but since it doesn't have Picasso's signature on it, it will not make anywhere near as much money. Some people might think his paintings look like children drew them, but if you gave them an original Picasso, they would probably hang it in their house and tell all their friends. That's the power of branding.

This branding is essentially what celebrities undergo.

This is why you have to become unique to create wealth. If I had sent you a one-page résumé claiming I was an Internet expert, you might have put this book aside. But by writing a book and getting you to read it, I have become unique in your eyes. A book is one way for me to establish authority as a leader in the Internet economy.

You, too, can become the go-to authority in your niche. If you are in the world of fashion, you have to identify the magazines and get them to write about you. You will then be seen as unique, not just another clothing brand.

You can research blogs and books in your niche, then write your own books and use them as your "Business Card 2.0." Books can be your calling card, which you can send to potential clients. You can use your Business Card 2.0 to attract media interest. A standard business card, résumé or brochure is much easier to create, but it is not unique. Only a few people take the time to create a book.

As the world becomes more competitive, you have to differentiate yourself. A few decades ago it was difficult to compete with Nike as TV advertising was expensive. Nike's founder established a brand, and became unique and an authority on athletic shoes. Consumers trusted Nike to provide high-quality shoes, so Nike could charge a higher price than a commodity shoe company.

Water was also a commodity until companies such as Nestlé and Evian came along. Now consumers pay different prices for brands of water.

If you want to create wealth for yourself, you have to treat yourself as a brand. Do you want to be just another film director? Or do you want to build a brand like Steven Spielberg has? Think about how you can start marketing yourself, so that people trust you and your films (or products and services).

Even companies such as Apple have celebrity CEOs like Steve Jobs who are brands in themselves. Telsa motors now has Elon Musk who gets as much publicity as his car company does. People in the internet economy often want to know as much about the founders or CEOs (e.g. Mark Zuckerberg, Bill Gates) as they do about the company whose product or service they are buying.

End Brandism

Branding is another reason why developed countries win and developing countries lose. If you were to put your money in a bank account, would you put it in a Swiss bank account or a Rwandan bank account? Would you buy a Swiss watch or a Vietnamese watch? The Swiss have made a name for themselves, even though not everybody Swiss is great at banking or watch making. Unfortunately, the brands of many emerging countries are not as powerful. You might be an amazing Yemeni software programmer, but since Yemen is not traditionally associated with superstar engineers, it is harder to sell yourself in the global market unless you can brand yourself better.

Like it or not, your name, gender, skin color and nationality are parts of your brand. You would have different ideas about this book if it were written by Tony Jones, Linda Jones, Tyrone Jackson, Heinz Schneider, Fatima Mohammed, Liu Chan or Deepak Patel, even if the content were the same. When we can't see people's physical appearance, we tend to stereotype them by the next best thing: their name.

You may wish to change your name for instance Andrew Warner of Mixergy.com found that his response was much better than when using Shuki Khalili as having an American sounding name got better responses. I also rebranded Amir Ahmad to Amir Anzur to give a more neutral branded and unique name. I found that Amir Ahmad was too common and not a "Googleable" name as there were so many Amir Ahmads – changing your name as I and many others have done might be a move you may want to consider. As harsh as it sounds it can dramatically increase your sales and wealth – who is likely to sell more Mark Smith or Mohammed Abdulla? You might not want to change your ethnicity but successful entrepreneur like Nazim Khan rebranded to James Caan and earned millions.

There is also negative branding. You might set up the best eCommerce site in the world, but if you are from Nigeria, customers might not trust you. Only a handful of Nigerians might scam people on the Internet, but the impact is felt by the other 167 million. Trust in the Nigerian brand plummets, making it harder for honest Nigerians to create wealth.

Every time there is negative news about your country in the global media, it impacts your business. Consumers and employers become more cautious about doing business with people of your nationality. Terrorist attacks in Pakistan might be carried out by just a handful of people, but the headlines make it harder for the other 180 million Pakistanis to get jobs, sell products and services or travel.

In the Middle East, Dubai has been able to create a powerful positive brand. An Internet startup from Dubai is more believable than one from Yemen, because people are more familiar with Dubai than Sana'a. This makes it easier for Dubai-based companies to do business than other cities in the region.

Be aware of what the place where you live says about you to the world. Help those around you to promote a more positive image for your city or country. You might want to make negative remarks about your leaders, but you could end up hurting your brand if international customers associate your country with its politicians. Bring positive change to where you live and highlight its success, rather than just reporting bad news (which traditional media love to do to attract more viewers/readers).

Places such as Dubai, Singapore and Switzerland are very controlled about the brand messages their countries give out so are often at a competitive advantage over countries that have completely free press.

You can beat brandism by letting people get to know you better. People tend to be brandist if they don't know someone. Once they get to know an individual, they tend to judge less. As you read this book, you are getting to know Amir Anzur, so I have already differentiated myself from the millions of other on the Internet.

I was able to break down stereotypes by getting you to read this book. You are now focused on my words and are less likely to care if I am short, fat, dark or white.

The great thing about the Internet is that it enables you to be judged for your work rather than your looks. In the real world people judge you on your weight or how you dress. Multinationals look at your work visa before hiring you. I call this passportism. I have hired people online as critical parts of our team (designers, programmers, editors) without even seeing a picture of them. As an entrepreneurs, I am more concerned about their output than their looks.

We stereotype to save ourselves time. It would take forever to get know a billion Chinese people, so we rely on the impressions we got from the last Chinese person we met or images we got from the media. Only if we visit the country would we be able to discover the Chinese are actually a billion individuals, not just one type.

We all stereotype because we don't have time to get to know everyone. It's a short cut, and as long as you don't box people in based on their nationality, you can use impressions to identify your expectations of someone. The point is to be aware of who you are and how others might perceive your brand.

Jobology

There was a time when you would write a one- or two-page résumé. If the employer liked your résumé, you could get a job interview, and be asked questions for an hour or so. If you passed the interview, you might be offered a job.

Through social networks such as Facebook, LinkedIn, Twitter, YouTube or your own website, you have the chance to differentiate yourself from the thousands of other people applying for the same job. Only 30% of jobs are found through advertisements or postings, which means 70% are found through networking. If you create enough of a brand for yourself, people will contact you.

Since you have more contacts through the web, your chances of hearing about a job are higher. Remember: Everything online says something about you. Like it or not, more and more employers will check your Facebook profile before hiring you. Even Facebook enables you to show off your talent.

Google receives over 20,000 résumés a week, but how many do you think are actually read? Are most of those résumés not a commodity? Building your personal online brand can make you unique so you can charge a higher amount for your services. Branding is critical to wealth creation.

If you are the best heart surgeon in the world, you will make much more money than an average heart surgeon. Specialists make more money than general practitioners because they have unique skills and are harder to find. Relatively few people may need to see a neurosurgeon, for example, but since there are so few of them, they can charge more for their services.

In London, taxi drivers known as black cabs make over $80,000 per year. The reason for their relatively high income? The city has a quota on the number of black-cab licenses. Since the supply is limited, these drivers charge more. Mobile apps such as Uber.com and TaxiBeat allow almost anyone to become a taxi driver and users can order them by phone. As the supply is increased of Taxi drivers the traditional taxi business are hurt.

A security guard working in New York can make $2,000 per month. The same guard with the same skills in Nepal could make only $100 per month. In the old economy, the New York guard's passport made him unique. If there were a true free economy, many Nepalese security guards would move to New York, driving salaries down to maybe $1,000 per month. But the U.S. government legislated that anyone working in their country has to make at least $7 per hour and pay taxes. They also controlled immigration so the New York security guard could keep his higher salary without fear of competition. Companies might have wanted to hire Nepalese guards, but since they didn't have U.S. work visas they couldn't.

Most online jobs are not limited by work visas. The uniqueness that came from simply being born in the right place is gone. People get jobs only if they deserve them.

If you asked me as an entrepreneur to choose between a book-cover designer based in New York who charged $1,000 or one based in Dhaka, Bangladesh who charged $100, I would, of course, choose the Bangladeshi, especially if his or her work was the same. Humans came up with the concepts of countries and segmentation; the Earth wasn't created that way. The Internet is breaking down those barriers.

It isn't simply that workers in poor countries are beating workers in rich countries on pricing. American, British and other developed country workers are increasingly also coming online. There are advantages they have such as often better communication skills as well as work ethic which enables someone from a small city like Manchester to get clients from New York.

Adam Smith, one of the fathers of modern economics, wrote *The Wealth of Nations* in the 1700s. He believed the division of labor or specialization was the key to creating wealth. The Internet allows you to specialize. You might be the best shoelace designer, but if there is no demand in your village, you can't make a living doing what you love. With the Internet, if you can brand yourself as "The greatest shoe lace designer in the world," you can create wealth. This specialization will attract a shoelace factory somewhere else that desperately wants to work with the greatest shoelace designer in the world.

If all of us have the same skills, the income we can earn will be limited. If we all have unique skills, the wealth we can create will be greater. On my team, for example, I might hire someone to video edit, another to write the book, another to market it and another to create a website. If all four were video editors, there would have no need for three of them, so I would just hire the cheapest.

COST TO SERVE

McDonald's became profitable because its food service processes allowed it to get more output per employee than its competitors. One employee could serve 100 customers in the time a competitor could deal with only 70. In the fast-food industry, labor is 70% of the cost, meaning McDonald's had more than a 40% lower cost-to serve.

Facebook has become one of the most valuable companies in the world because its costs to serve are lower. Compare Facebook to a magazine. Both business models are built around advertising to readers.

Journalists write articles for a magazine, photographers take pictures, and editors put the content together. Then there are advertising salespeople and printing costs. Distributors get paid to take the magazines to the newsstands, cashiers to sell them.

Facebook gets people like you and I to provide status updates and pictures for free. You are journalist, photographer and editor, but you are not even getting paid for it! There are no costs to print Facebook and content storage costs are getting cheaper every year, dropping by half every two years. Advertisers don't need salespeople to convince them of the right place for their ads. The segmentation of the market users wants to aim for is up to them.

Instead of translating the magazine into several languages, users automatically update their statuses in their own language; the Portuguese see content in Portuguese, the French see it in French, and the Arabs sees it in Arabic.

Facebook can do all this with fewer than 3,000 employees. All that content for over 1.2 billion people, updated 24 hours a day, 365 days a year. In the native tongue. No TV station, newspaper or radio station has even a tenth of Facebook's audience, yet many employ many times the number of staff.

This self-service model has benefited many companies. Take a bank, for instance. A few decades ago the only way to check your bank balance was to go to a cashier. The advent of automatic teller machines (ATMs) meant the bank did not need to employ as many cashiers. ATMs still need to be installed and maintained in many locations, though. With the Internet, people can serve themselves. The bank saves a lot of money since it doesn't need to pay cashiers. There is less demand for ATMs since you can access your account from your home computers.

The same goes for travel arrangements. You enter your name, address and credit card number and select a flight. You don't need an agent to do this. This saves the airlines the cost to serve you. They can keep this money as additional profit or pass on savings to their customers. The consumer gets lower costs, less chance of error and much quicker service, which is available 24 hours a day, seven days a week, from anywhere.

Online retailers have also lowered their costs to serve. In the traditional economy, building a bookstore in a shopping mall cost a lot of money. Then you had to pay rent and electricity and hire staff. You probably lost a lot of money through theft, too, and 70% of that came from your own employees. Amazon can serve its customers from one large warehouse in a remote area with cheaper rent and less staff. The savings are passed on to customers.

The Internet also lowers the costs to employ people. For instance, if you lived in the UAE pre-Internet and wanted to hire a video editor, you would need to search the Subcontinent, pay for candidates' flights, obtain their work visas and provide them with accommodation. Then, and only then, could they get to work on your video. Now you can go to websites such as upwork.com or eLance.com and hire people directly. If you live in a town with a few thousand people, it would be difficult to find an amazing software programmer, especially one willing to work for a minimal wage. Now, you can easily find great talent in a different part of the world.

To review: the population of Switzerland is 8 million. A haircut there costs $45. The population of Pakistan is 180 million. A haircut there costs $1. The Swiss education system is much better than Pakistan's, and a few decades ago this would have been a huge advantage for, say, a computer programmer. But now, Pakistanis can access MIT's website (www.mit.edu), get all the university's lectures for free, and learn to code. If they need to get their math up to snuff, they can visit www.KhanAcademy. org and get lessons from kindergarten through Grade 12 for free. A Swiss software company can choose prospective employees from Pakistan, India, the Philippines, Kenya or Egypt at a fraction of the cost. You can educate them and have them working at the productivity of a local in no time. Then you can pass on the savings to your customers or increase your profit margins.

Nike's founder, Phil Knight, is a billionaire because he was able to get Americans to perform high-value work (creating ads, sponsoring Tiger Woods and Michael Jordan) while having low-level work (stitching shoes) done in places such as Indonesia and Vietnam. The consumer got a great product at a reasonable price and so the cost to serve was lowered. You can apply the lessons of Nike to your own cost cutting, by hiring some talent locally and some from a different part of the world. For instance, Indians might want to hire American voice-over talent so their videos sound more professional, while Americans might want to hire data-entry operators from India.

As the world becomes more globalized, many talented people in emerging countries will make far more than untalented people in developed countries. The talent, and the marketing of that talent, rather than the color of one's passport will be the key to wealth creation.

Business can happen only once trust is established between two people. Before the Internet, it took time to get to know strangers and establish trust.

In the book *Three Cups of Tea*, author Greg Mortenson quotes a village chief:

"Here [in Pakistan and Afghanistan], we drink three cups of tea to do business; the first you are a stranger, the second you become a friend, and the third, you join our family, and for our family we are prepared to do anything – even die."

- Haji Ali, Korphe village chief, Karakoram Mountains, Pakistan

The Internet enables you to do business by drinking two cups of tea instead of three. People can learn about you by researching you online. You don't have to repeat yourself; once you start increasing your Web presence, people across the world will feel they know you. This ultimately saves you time, as trust is instantly established so business can happen quicker.

Blogging and writing this book for me is like having a cup of tea with people. Once you read it, you feel you can trust me more. We don't have to spend as much time getting to know each other, which means less time with lawyers and more time doing business. Facebook and twitter updates also helps me to grow relationships with people online.

More and more people work as freelance agents now. Developing relationships cost these people time, which is, of course, a cost. Once a freelancer's brand is established on the Internet, the time he or she needs to start business relationships decreases, saving everyone involved money.

Summary of the Simple Wealth Formula

Let's revisit the Simple Wealth Formula:

Amount of Value You Can Add

X	Number of People You Can Impact
–	Number of People Who Can Do What You Do
–	Cost to Serve
=	Total Wealth Created

You can see how simple wealth creation is. You create value for the world by doing what you do best (hairstyling, graphic design, computer programming, making hamburgers, entertaining or educating). The Internet gives you more tools to do things yourself or connect with people who can help you.

You have to appeal to as many people as possible, and thanks to the Internet, three of the seven billion people on the planet world are connected. You need to be unique, to differentiate yourself from the other seven billion. And through the Web you have more opportunities to find your niche and establish relationships. There might be others who can do your job as good, if not better, but you can create a brand that people trust and want to be associated with.

Great brands such as Louis Vuitton, Nike and Rolex took decades to create, and you, too, will have to think of the long term. Connect with your fellow students while you are still in school, as they are your customers, suppliers or business partners of the near future. A brand is created one person at a time, and your friends see you as a brand, too.

Finally, look to decrease your cost to serve. You do not have to buy everything locally because there is great talent around the world available to help you at the click of a mouse. There are also many tools on the Internet that can drastically save you time and money.

6. THE GAMIFICATION OF LIFE

In the previous chapter you learned how wealth in terms of money is created. In this chapter you will learn that not everyone is playing the same game.

In the world of computer science there is a concept known as *gamification*. Computer Scientists try and put some gamification inside their websites so that people are more attracted to revisit their websites and use more of their services. For instance, Facebook has gamification built in as every time you post a picture or status update you want to check back on the website to see who and how many people have liked or commented on your update. This simple game of having a number of likes associated with a comment displayed publicly means that Facebook keeps attracting visitors back to its website.

Grown men and women across the world post statuses that they hope will attract as many likes as possible. This gives their ego satisfaction. People will post their videos on YouTube and keep checking back to see how many views they got. They will tweet to see how many retweets they got.

Games Societies Play

Successful corporations build gamification into their organization so that people know how to get further ahead in their careers. When I worked for Accenture, a firm with over 200,000 employees, we knew that we would start at Analyst level, if we worked hard and fulfilled requirements such as training and billable hours we would move up to consultant, then manager, senior manager and eventually Partner or executive director. Each level had its requirements and it wasn't just the money increase that we chased but also the job title and the prestige that brought with it.

The gamification helps corporations to grow. It helps websites to keep attracting users.

In this same way societies have gamification built into them. Try and think through what it takes for you to become "successful" in your society. It might not necessarily be making money. There are other ways to gain respect such as showing your religious virtues, a happy family, an industry award, fame, or simply doing your job well whether it is as a teacher or a nurse.

While going for a jog in Islamabad, Pakistan I took my Smartphone with me. I have the Nike Running App which told me the exact route I take on a GPS system, the number of calories burned and the total distance run. I ran into another lady who was carrying a counter with her. I asked her what that was for – she replied that it was to count the number of times she says the name of God as she goes for her walk.

American society has built in success in this world. Pakistani society has built in success in the after world. The only challenge being that it is hard to actually know the score whereas metrics such as weight, bank account etc. are easier to measure.

American society has wealth creation built into its DNA. Heroes are created of people like Bill Gates, Steve Jobs and Mark Zuckerberg who have become billionaires. Places such as Silicon Valley make it easier to build a billion dollar company. Remember that once you launch your big idea you will need to be heard - this is the problem that most Internet startups face - the ability to be heard.

As the focus of Silicon Valley is on innovation and new ideas, a business that starts there has more access to finance, experience and media to become successful globally. The same rules for making a company successful might not be applicable where you live. Companies such as YouTube, Twitter, Amazon were actually losing money while being valued at billions of dollars. YouTube for instance was losing $15 million per month when Google acquired it for $1.62 billion.

American society has many magazines such as Time, Forbes, Fortune and Entrepreneur that write about companies and entrepreneurs. Forbes tells us who the richest people in the world are so the gamification keeps heroes of entrepreneurs. Most other societies do not have as much attention paid to their entrepreneurs so entrepreneurs have less of a chance to become celebrities or promote their products and services. This in turn inspires less people to go out and start a business.

AmirAnzur.com, Dean, WebpreneurAcademy.com, Chief Simplification Officer, aartec.com

Now though marketing is becoming easier at a global level. You can take out advertising based from wherever you are and target people wherever they live. Websites such as YouTube, Facebook, LinkedIn, Google all offer some sort of advertising programme where you can pick your audience based on geography or activities they liked or are members of or even websites they have visited. Of course paid advertising is not as good as having media publications write about you for free.

One thing that is hard to imagine when you come from a poor part of the world is how many rich people there are in the world. As you are surrounded by poor people you imagine no one would pay the higher prices but in fact because there are so many people online there are buyers ready to buy your things if the service and quality are there.

You can treat the concept of earning online as a game - calculating how many visitors you get, how many actually buy, how many are satisfied, how many buy again from you.

American media glorifies business. Television shows and magazines talk about the stock market, interview entrepreneurs, teach personal development to help them progress in life.

In Pakistan the development is towards religion. The only challenge with the game of religion is that it is hard to tell who has the authority to speak on it or who has what score. In the world of business it is easy to see profits, stock price and other figures that are harder to dispute. With religion just because someone has the perceived authority due to age, dress or some other sort the gamification can lead to people chasing different things in the world.

So one of the major reasons for terrorism is that different games are being played. Some societies are chasing wealth. Others are not aware about how wealth is created or whether it is the game they want to play and hence we have collisions of cultures.

The trick is to become aware of the games. If you are working in a corporation you need to be aware that the quarterly numbers need to be met. You need to know what the rules are for getting promoted or gaining more wealth for your company or yourself. If you are in a society where religion is the game than you need to be aware of what rules you need to follow. How you can climb up the social structures or points of life.

I went out to teach wealth creation in Pakistan but eventually realized that the society has different structure than American society. There is a reason why Americans are more successful online than Pakistanis and indeed most of the rest of the world – the society is built for internet success.

Games Facebookers Play

Gamification happens in facebook and other social networking websites where some people will try to impress everyone on how well their careers are going, how attractive their spouse is, how physically active they are or a number of different human games being played. Remember that you can help them "win" by simply hitting the "like" button or commenting on their success. Social media is not only about you but about others feeling important.

Remember to not get stuck in the games but become aware of where you are participating. When building your idea and bringing it to market see how you can build gamification into it so it becomes more addictive to people. Take a few minutes to observe what games you have unconsciously become a player in. What games are played in your society - some examples on social media games are:

- "How wealthy have I become" - showing vacations, cars, houses or other toys
- "How happy is our family" - Happy, smiley pictures of family
- "How much bad luck do I have" - Down on luck status updates
- "How religious am I" - people that want to show how passionate they are about their religion
- "How much of a workaholic am I"- Mentioning how much work you are doing
- "How my life is fun" - Taking pictures doing activities like sky diving etc.

Social media and the Internet are bringing games into our lives whether we like it or not. You for instance, have become a celebrity whether you chose to or not and every message you send is probably directed to the game you are playing. More and more of your life is observed by others. Do you want that or not?

Societies such as Pakistan are having a harder time adjusting to the Internet as it is bringing in values and insights to the society that were never possible before. Pakistan essentially had a monopoly of religion where people were taught that they were special due to the religion they were born into. There was never a challenge to another point of view. Along comes the Internet with its infamous freedom of speech and now as some people criticize religion so the country doesn't know what to do except shut down all of YouTube or block websites.

Arab governments faced what became known as the Arab spring as people were able to gather and criticize their leaders as they were never able to before. Some societies such as China are better prepared for the Internet as they have invested massive amounts of resources on their censorship so the rules of the game are different in China.

As I started Webpreneur Academy I realised that in the game of education where you come from is important so I chose a city which had positive brand association - London - to be the home of Webpreneur Academy. Your country should also realise the critical importance the brand has in helping its citizens gain a competitive advantage when starting an Internet business. Countries and cities must brand themselves with positive brand association so that their citizens find it easier to sell products and services.

It is not a good or bad thing to be caught in games. It is just to be aware of the games and to know exactly how to win those games that you must be aware of.

Which games are you playing?

Pakonomics: Why Americans are Rich and Pakistanis even richer

One question I wanted to answer when I started this journey online is why there is a difference of wealth in the US where an average American makes over $50,000 per year and in Pakistan where an average Pakistani makes less than $1,500 per year.

One of the reasons I found is that different games are being played in the societies. Americans have the game of Wealth creation. This is one of the main reasons that Donald Trump become president. He was able to show that he was "winning" the game by showing his private jets and his wealth and beautiful wife and family. He had become a billionaire and thus a "success".

Pakistanis are playing a different game. Religion is a lot more important and so it is "how to get into heaven". Which means things like being a good person, saying your prayers, fasting during Ramadan etc.

These are different games from each other so once I realized that actually a Pakistani Uber driver might actually sacrifice his income to work less hours during Ramadan or clock off work to say his prayers.

You just have to be careful though as in the competitive world if you don't provide the best service someone else will.

Consumerism doesn't necessarily lead to happiness.

"Advertising has us chasing cars and clothes, working jobs we hate so we can buy stuff we don't need."

- Chuck Palahniuk, Fight Club

At its core what people are telling you to create wealth online is to sell something to someone. So you might just decide this is not the game you want to play!

7. FOUR TYPES OF WEALTH CREATORS

In the book *Rich Dad, Poor Dad*, authors Robert Kiyosaki and Sharon Lechtor talk about the four types of wealth creators:

1. **Employee** – these people have a standard salary and a job working for someone else.

2. **Self-Employed** – these are the doctors or lawyers who run their own practice. But if they are ever ill or don't turn up to work, they don't make money.

3. **Business Owners** – these are the people such as Bill Gates and Steve Jobs who create their own businesses.

4. **Investors** – these are people such as Warren Buffett who have money work for them by purchasing a stake in other businesses.

You can create wealth no matter what category you are in, but some have more limitations. If you are already on a career path, determine who the richest employee is and how much money you could make in that job. You will find there is usually a limit to what you can earn. Being an employee has many benefits, not least of which is a stable income every month. If you love what you do, being an employee is a good category to be in.

Self-employed people love the freedom of being their own boss. They can choose the hours they work and the activities they want to do. The only problem with most self-employed people or freelancers is that they have limited ability to scale. Again, if they are ill, they are not likely to earn money. If they want to double their income, they need to work double the hours or double their rates.

Business owners can start to scale their products and services. Ray Kroc, the McDonald's founder, was not the hamburger chef at his restaurant. Instead he created the **systems and processes** that allowed his hamburgers to be served around the world. He made a little bit from each hamburger sold. This category is where the likes of Richard Branson, Steve Jobs and Bill Gates fall into.

Investors have their money work for them. For instance, they give a startup $10,000 for a 20% stake in the company.

The Internet helps all groups create more wealth. Employees can find better jobs by searching sites such as LinkedIn to see who works at the company they want to work at, connect with them and send in their résumé. They can use the internet not only to brand themselves in their micro-niche industries so that they are valued more by their employers but can also use the internet to continuously learn more about their subject.

The self-employed have better marketing opportunities. Using sites such as Facebook, the self-employed can make sure they are not forgotten. If you are friends with your dentist and every time you log in to your Facebook account you see his or her dental tip, you are not likely to forget the person for your next visit. For the self-employed, it is important to be seen as an authority in their niche. Would you go to the average dentist or the best dentist you could afford?

The self-employed can attract more customers by providing free educational content. A dentist can set up a system that shows a weekly three-minute video on how to take care of your teeth. Although the dentist is giving free advice, it is really a form of marketing. Customers are more likely to visit a dentist they know and trust and more likely to recommend him or her to their friends. The video helps build the dentist's clientele.

Business owners primarily use the Web to market their company. They also use the Web to hire and train their employees, reducing costs by hiring globally or using software to manage more and more of their business, allowing them to create systems and processes so customers do more of the work themselves (e.g., booking an airline ticket online rather than through an agent) and monitor employees (e.g., monitoring sales performance through tools such as Salesforce.com).

People who might not have had a chance to invest a few decades ago can now afford to. To buy a McDonald's franchise costs anywhere from $500,000 to $1 million. Then you have to rent space, hire staff and buy furniture. Now you can start an online business with a few hundred dollars. If you live in a richer part of the world, you might invest in a startup in a poorer part of the world because of the price difference.

When your idea begins to work, you can then scale it to a richer part of the world.

This is where a big shift in the economy is happening. People with safe jobs making a decent living are investing in ventures around the world. In the old economy, people such as Warren Buffet would buy shares in publicly traded companies on the New York Stock Exchange. He influenced decisions and made a profit if they grew.

You, too, can now search out entrepreneurs in a different part of the world, invest money and take a stake in the company. Once the idea proves itself in one niche it can grow. If you are looking for investors, you need to create a Web presence to convince potential partners. People do not like to invest in strangers, but they will invest in entrepreneurs they believe in. Instead of investing $10,000 in a huge company such as Google or General Electric in which they have no control over the direction of the company, they can invest $10,000 in a smaller company and have more input. Sites like www.CrowdCube.com exist that enable entrepreneurs to find investors. A friend of mine Natali Stajcic raised $225,000 for her company selling The Pressery – almond based drinks. She gave shares in her company in return for money that she will use to start and grow her company.

Companies have become cheaper and cheaper to start, making it possible for more and more ordinary people to invest. The returns can be huge but the company can take years to get off the ground. The Internet enables more people to become investors or business owners, which is where true wealth is possible. The collaboration of developing-world entrepreneurs and developed-world part-time investors is going to be a bigger trend. More regular employees in developed-world countries will set aside $500 to $1,000 per month to hire intelligent, driven entrepreneurs in developed countries to produce products and services for their part of the world. Normal people with jobs will set aside their income investing in projects which could create substantial wealth for them.

An easy way to start a business is to look for a problem to solve. What software or service could solve a problem in your part of the world? If you have a few hundred dollars to spare, you can hire and train someone from an emerging country to work on your problem. It's usually more fun to have a stake in a startup than a boring bank account accruing less than 5% interest.

8. HOW TO CLONE YOURSELF

A few thousand years ago if you discovered how to start a fire you would call people around you and demonstrate it live. This limited the number of people you could tell about your new knowledge since you would always have to be there. There was only one of you, so you were limited to the places that you could travel. Knowledge tended to stay local.

A few hundred years later, humans discovered how to draw. You could now create cave drawings to show others how to start a fire. You didn't have to be there; you had effectively cloned yourself. People could come to your cave at their own convenience and get instructions on how to start a fire. Your cave drawings taught, even when you were not there.

Eventually we discovered pen and paper and could handwrite instructions and communicate discoveries to different parts of the world. Writing by hand was a slow process, but Johannes Guttenberg made it cheaper and more accessible in the 1440s when he invented the printing press. Now you could write your instructions once, and millions could receive your knowledge.

The radio came along in the early 1900s, and your message could now be broadcast to millions, who could listen while they went about their daily chores.

By the 1930s, TV was invented and now you could give a live demonstration of how to start a fire. People could actually see you. An even better clone had been created.

The printing press was relatively local. There was a cost associated with printing so you would need to ensure there was enough of a need before you went to press. While you could now send your message to more people, you still had to pay distribution costs.

Radio and TV stations also had costs. There was the cost of recording and the cost to transmit the signal across the country. There were only a limited number of licenses given, and since governments meted them out, you had to be careful what you said.

Few TV, radio stations or newspapers were truly global. If you were Nigerian and living in South Africa, it was unlikely you could listen to your favorite Nigerian radio station. If you could not be at home at 9 p.m. to watch your favorite TV show, that was it. Unless you had someone to record it for you the show was gone forever.

By the mid-1990s, the Internet became available to the general public. It was a combination of the printing press, radio and TV, and, even better, you could communicate with it. You could type your fire demonstration into a word processor, download it on a podcast for people to listen to in their cars, or videotape and upload it to YouTube. If your audience got confused at any time, they could email you or leave a comment on YouTube.

Your cave could be anywhere in the world, and you could communicate with anyone. Advancements in technology effectively allowed you to clone yourself.

Printing presses and radio and TV stations have gatekeepers. Resources are limited; there are only so many pages in a newspaper. Only one radio or TV show can be broadcast at a time. The gatekeepers — newspaper editors and radio and TV programmers — decided who was good enough to go on air and the content that would appeal to readers, listeners or viewers.

If the editor of a newspaper didn't think your ability to start a fire was a story worth printing, there was little hope of you getting your idea across to the world. If a publisher didn't feel your book was any good, it wouldn't get printed and your ideas could not spread.

When the Internet came, space and time scarcities were erased. Now there was unlimited room to print your story (over 200 million blog posts are written every day). A site such as YouTube allows anyone to post almost any content (over 300 hours of video are posted every minute).

You no longer have to pitch to the gatekeepers, but can go straight to your audience. Most big media stars used to live in places such as Hollywood or New York City, since the gatekeepers lived there. Among American teenagers YouTube creators were found to be more popular than mainstream celebrities.

Salespeople realize how important relationships are. The more people, who know, like and trust you, the more you are likely to sell. In the old economy you would make relationships one at a time. In the Internet age, though, you can clone yourself. You can update all your friends at once on where you are and what you are doing on Facebook. In the old economy, you limited your friends since you didn't have time to keep up with too many. With more friends online, you can educate them on your products and services.

In essence, convincing people to buy is about educating them about your product's or service's benefits. Many of you who read this book, for instance, will become more interested in the web and take a WebpreneurAcademy.com course to learn more.

Steve Jobs cloned himself by launching new products on multiple platforms. Many who watched his demonstrations on their computer screens went out and bought the product. The only problem with cloning is that most of us never took media-training classes. Until a decade ago, you never had to appear in photos or on TV unless you really wanted to. Now, almost anywhere you go, someone has a phone camera and can post a picture of you on Facebook or Instagram.

Let's say you wanted to learn basic trigonometry pre-Internet. If you were lucky and had a good teacher, a small enough classroom and enough confidence, you could ask your teacher about concepts you didn't understand.

If you had a lousy teacher, a huge classroom or lacked confidence, you lost out. You would fall behind in trigonometry, which would have an impact on your next class and the class after that. You might begin to feel stupid, lose your confidence and you would fall even farther behind.

Teachers have been able to clone themselves and spread their knowledge using the Internet. Sal Khan founded KhanAcademy.org after his nephews wanted some extra math tutoring. He wasn't in the same city, so he recorded a few lessons and sent them the link to YouTube. Before long, other kids started watching the lessons, and Khan went on to record over 2,000 video lectures covering everything from kindergarten to Grade 12. Kids can watch the lessons at their own pace, and replay them until they understand the concepts. They can visit forums, ask questions and get even more help. If they don't understand a concept in the way one teacher explains it, they can seek out a different teacher for the same concept.

The rate of innovation will get even faster. A few thousand years ago before cavemen figured out how to spread their ideas, the innovations would be local. As society progressed, people could connect, but their messages were still filtered by gatekeepers. Now people across the world can share their knowledge and build on others' knowledge so that everyone can innovate.

As we read in the chapter for wealth creation, more knowledge can lead to more value and more wealth. Someone who is educated is likely to be a user of shovels rather than teaspoons. Education used to be formal, take place in schools and depended on exams. In the Internet economy, you can learn from millions of teachers online without having to take an exam or go to school.

The quality of teachers has improved, too, since the best can clone. At the moment, most lessons are in English, but as more people come online from other countries, they will be more content in Swahili, Arabic, Korean, Hindi and Urdu. If you want to truly help your community, you, too, will need to become a Sal Khan or an Amir Anzur. Instead of teaching a few kids in a classroom, you can reach millions from your home.

I runs classes online. I have researched wealth- creation content over the past few years that I believe every teenager and adult should understand. I have live sessions in which students from places such as Singapore, New York, London, Delhi, Abu Dhabi, Sydney and Tokyo ask me questions on launching their businesses. Students can all look at the same website at the same time, something that was not possible more than a decade ago.

This ability to clone themselves across the world in the new economy will create a lot of wealth for not only salespeople, but also for teachers who would have been able to work with a limited number of students in the past. In the knowledge economy more and more people will seek knowledge and hence teaching will be an even bigger industry especially for specialized knowledge.

9. SIX WEAPONS OF INFLUENCE

If you want to create wealth online you will have to sell something to someone. One of the best books written on sales is "Influence: Science and practice" by Robert Cialdini.

Cialdini spent many years researching the world of sales and discovered six core weapons of influence. I found that these same principals apply to the online world as well and if you understand them you will be better positioned to win in the internet economy.

1. Authority

As humans we respect authority. If an expert says something than it must be true. This is why you might see actors wearing dentist coats while advertising toothpaste on television.

If you are also trying to get people to buy from you, you must be perceived as the authority on that subject. Those that are perceived as experts get paid more and are in more demand.

There are a number of ways you can gain authority in your field. Writing a book is an example. It is no coincidence that the word "authority" has "author" in it. I am not walking about an ebook but a physical book. In the old economy this was very difficult to get published – in the internet economy though you can visit a site like CreateSpace.com or Lulu.com and upload your word document which will get printed on demand. You can then order 30 to 50 copies and send them out to perspective clients or media.

Appearing on television or traditional newspapers and magazines will also increase your authority. You can then take your appearances on television and put them on your website. A slower but effective way to get authority might be to get a PhD from a university in the field that you want to be perceived as an authority.

Companies like Nike win a bigger share of the marketshare as they have authorities like Tiger Woods, Michael Jordan or other leading athletes wear their shoes and clothing. If someone who is the best in their sport uses their products than they must be the best is what customers perceive.

I build authority by updating my twitter, facebook or linkedin with statuses relevant to my field – internet entrepreneurship. I have also appeared on television and been featured in newspapers.

I noticed authority being used in religion. Religious scholars dress a certain way. There is a scholar in India with millions of followers called Dr. Zakir Naik. I tried to understand why he had such a big following as I always try to follow people with a following. He had memorized at least three of the holy books and would answer any question with authority. If people wanted to get into heaven they know that he is more likely to help them get there.

2. Reciprocity

As humans we like to do for others as what they have done for us. Human society has give and take built into them. A salesman might buy their clients lunch but there is an unwritten obligation that the client will give the salesman business.

In the 1970s the Hari Krishnas were a group of people struggling to raise money for their cause in the United States. They started using the reciprocity principal to increase donations to their cause. They would meet people in airports or train stations and offer them a flower. People would often say "no thanks" but they would insist and say "its for you, it's a gift". People would hesitantly take the flower.

They would walk a few feet further and there would be another Hari Krishna with a bucket saying "donations...donations". As the person had taken a free flower they would often feel obliged to donate – often significantly more than the cost of the flower.

What Cialdini discovered is that there was another Hari Krishna who would go through recollect the flowers thrown away by the customers a few feet away to recycle through to the gift giver. The gift strategy significantly increased the donations to the Hari Krishna's cause.

In the online world internet marketers will often give a "free" report, book or video in exchange for an email address. This then leads them to build relationships with their potential customers. They send a few emails with valuable information and then eventually ask for a small sale or some sort. There might be free shampoo samples in the post or free seminars which educators give in return they expect a few people will signup.

3. Scarcity

We want what we can't have. As something gets more rare our desire for it increases. This is why Ferrari limits the number of cars it sells every year so that demand outstrips supply. Apple does this with its product launches so that people wait for hours for the new iPhone as they know that it will run out if they don't get it now.

Internet entrepreneurs also build in scarcity to their products or services for instance having a count down timer for when offers expire or limiting the number of products they sell – even though it would not cost them any more to enable more customers to purchase from them.

4. Social Proof

Most humans are like sheep – they will do what others are doing. We need social proof to convince us to take a certain path. When Apple first launched the iPod sales were helped by the fact that they had unique white colored earphones which showed other consumers that the consumer had an iPod.

You can use social proof by having your customers say something nice about your products and post it on your website. Social proof is also visible by the number of views a video has or followers an account has. Many people online often fake these numbers online by "buying" fans or having some algorithms increase their numbers but that is getting harder to do as sites like Facebook, YouTube and twitter get more intelligent with their algorithms.

5. Likeability

All things being equal we like doing business with those we like. This is why companies with likeable CEOs like Steve Jobs, Mark Zuckerberg or Bill Gates benefit as they give a personality to a business.

Network marketing – often called "pyramid selling" – works well as people end up selling to their friends.

You too will likely get your first few customers from your friends or friends of friends.

6. Commitment and Consistency

We like to be consistent to what we have committed. This is why sales people will often ask us a bunch of questions to get small agreements before asking for the actual sale. They might ask "you would like a car that is good value for money", "you liked driving this car", "your family likes the car", "the car is within your budget." and then finally go ahead with a commitment like "would you like me to book this car for you.". As there were a series of small commitments people are more likely to commit to buying the car.

There was a restaurant in Chicago that had a high number of people that didn't turn up when they booked a table for diner. The restaurant manager simply asked "will you call us if you can't make the reservation." And simply because the customer said "yes I will call" there were less likely to have a no-show at the restaurant.

Internet entrepreneurs build sales funnels online. They start by selling a small priced item to their customer. They then sell the same customer a higher priced item and eventually an even higher value item. The customers come online with small commitments which grow overtime.

Influence and persuasion are critical skills for the internet economy. Take some of the above methods to keep an eye out on how you are being influenced. Develop your own methods to ethically convince people to buy from you.

10. LESSONS IN WEALTH FROM PRE-INTERNET AGE

They say history repeats itself, so what are the lessons we can learn from people who created great wealth in the past century? In this chapter we list some wealth creators. If you have not heard of these people or companies, we recommend you familiarize yourself with them; obviously the Internet makes it easier for you to research!

OPRAH WINFREY

Oprah Winfrey became a billionaire and one of the highest-paid entertainers of the last century, building a brand that many knew, like and trusted. If Oprah lost all her money today, she could become a millionaire again almost overnight. She could partner with almost anyone to promote a product and get a share of the revenues.

If Oprah were to approach me and offer to promote this book in exchange for half the proceeds, I would gladly agree, because any book Oprah promotes makes it onto the best-seller list within a few weeks. She could have the same deal with other producers.

You can become the new Oprah Winfrey. A Chicago TV station gave her the chance to communicate through her talk show. You have YouTube, and do not need anybody's permission to start your own show. YouTube actually has a bigger global reach than any TV station that Oprah was on when she started her career.

You do not have to be living in Chicago or Los Angeles to connect with big celebrities. You can sign up for Skype and start contacting celebrities in your niche. If you have a large following or are good at interviewing, many will be happy to talk to you. You can record the conversation and upload it to YouTube. Skype is free. Connecting to celebrities is free. YouTube is free.

Interviewing authors (usually looking to promote their books) or businesspeople (looking for promote their businesses) not only gives you great content, but also is a great way to learn from the best. Over time, you will build up a network of influential people.

Building a following takes time, which you have. Oprah did her show for 25 years to build up her loyal following. You need to start somewhere, but within a few years you will have built up a following, which will result in wealth. When you build a following, you become much more important to society. Oprah has probably had more influence on American culture and society than most presidents who served during that time.

I often get approached with free products, services and even sponsorships, just to promote things to my followers. Once you become a person of influence, more and more people will ask you to help promote their products and services. Oprah did not become famous overnight. Many people start on the Internet, don't see immediate results, and give up. Creating wealth on the Internet is a marathon, with many sprints in the middle. If you want to be in this game be prepared for the long term.

HOW TV CREATED WEALTH

Think of an actor working a few hundred years ago – before TV came along, the Tom Cruise of the 1800s. The only way for the old Tom Cruise to make more money would be to perform to a packed house every night.

There were three problems with this business model. First, the old Tom Cruise would have to continually perform if he wanted to make money. If he ever fell ill or wanted to take a day off, he could not make money.

Old Tom's target market was limited. He would work on Broadway, so his audience was limited to the couple of thousand New Yorkers who could fill the theater. If he wanted more people to see him perform he would have to tour different cities, and since those people hadn't seen him before, he would have to build his brand from scratch each time.

The old Tom would be stuck doing the same thing over and over again. If he wanted to work on another play, someone else would perform his old role — and make money doing it.

Thanks to TV and cinema, the Tom Cruise of the 1980s had a much easier time creating his wealth. All he had to do was act once. He could work on every scene until he got it just right. And then relax. If he fell ill or took a few days off, *Top Gun* could still be seen around the world. All he had to do is visit a few TV shows to help promote his movies. When he started working on his next movie, the old ones still made money for him.

Oprah Winfrey, Jerry Springer, Steven Spielberg, the cast of *Friends* and a whole lot of other celebrities have TV to thank for helping them create vast fortunes.

The Internet will amplify the effect of TV. Now you don't need to be based in Hollywood to be able to clone yourself. People can produce content that can be seen everywhere and forever. Your movie can be seen at any time, rather than the times set by a TV network or film distributors. Revenues models are changing so that you can make money from advertising or charge people to watch online.

Creative people around the world have a greater opportunity than at any time in history to make money, thanks to the Internet. The number of millionaires that TV generated will be a mere fraction of the number the Internet creates over the next few decades. But you will need to be creative, not only with your filmmaking or songwriting, but also with your business model.

You don't even need a broadcasting license to start your own TV channel. The Tom Cruises of the world will have a lot of competition from "nobodies" like you and us over the next few decades.

It is easier to learn the impact of a new technology by seeing how a similar technology impacted history. Knowing about a change that is coming, and taking advantage of it, however, are two different things.

HOW MCDONALD'S CREATED WEALTH

With over $24 billion of sales per year and 400,000 employees serving over 33,000 restaurants worldwide, McDonald's has become one of the most successful companies. It generated wealth by creating a system that looked beyond an individual restaurant. You can pay McDonald's to franchise its name and it will give you a system for picking a location, training your employees and serving food.

Wealth creation is about creating systems. As you build your business in the Internet economy, how can you build systems so your business can grow? The Internet allows you to systemize things so you don't need to always be there. For instance, Webpreneur Academy is our teaching system. Teachers in the old economy make much less money because they are not scaling their knowledge; they always have to be in their classrooms.

LESSONS FROM AMERICA

The U.S. is the wealthiest country in the world. One in four dollars spent around the world is done so by an American. I am not suggesting everyone follow the country's business model, but examine some of the factors that enabled it to succeed in some things.

One of the keys to success is great communication infrastructure. The U.S. built roads, railways and airports as well as TV and radio stations. If you were an entrepreneur and had an idea, you had plenty of methods to spread your word. One of the reasons the top Internet companies (Yahoo, Google, Facebook, eBay, etc.) are all based in California is the amount of media coverage there. *The Social Network* generated millions of dollars of publicity for Facebook, for example. Many Hollywood movies show an Apple in the background, which familiarizes audiences with the computer and helps the company gain market share. America has a culture of cross-promotion.

Notice, for instance, magazines such as *Time* and *Newsweek* often mention Apple or Microsoft in their stories. If you are based in a country such as Afghanistan, you do not have many newspapers or websites, so there are fewer people communicating about your product. Abdulla the Afghan might have created Facebook before Mark Zuckerberg came up with the idea, but Zuckerberg had the benefit of the U.S. media, which spread the word about his product. Abdulla could share his with only a few dozen of his (non-influential) friends.

The U.S. is also diverse. You might be roommates with an Italian- American or go to school with an African-American or date an Arab- American. Diversity leads to many different points of view, which leads to innovation.

American culture is also less risk-averse. In many Arab countries, for instance, people have to be careful what our family thinks. They must consider their family's honor before they do anything too drastic. In the U.S., this is less the case. Michael Jackson got more publicity for his odd behavior than a "normal" person would. The publicity helped him sell records and become more famous. Americans take more risks and come up with crazy products and services – some work and many don't. Failure is accepted as a process of innovation.

America also has a large population that speaks the same language. If you have a cool idea, it can spread quickly to 300 million people. Every town has multiple McDonald's, Wal-Marts, Starbucks and other franchises. Coca-Cola sells to McDonald's, which is available across the U.S.

Telecommunication was relatively cheap in America. Long-distance calls were cheaper than in other countries, which made it easier to do business domestically and internationally. Travel was also cheap and the workforce very mobile. It was not a problem to move from New York City to Los Angeles if someone had a better job opportunity. People in emerging countries often think more about leaving their families to settle in a different city, even if it's in their own country.

The rest of the world now has many of the advantages the U.S. had a few decades ago thanks to the Internet. If you wanted to become an author in Oman, for instance, you had an audience of three million, at most. Now, you can sell to over 350 million Arab speakers through the Web.

Phones are much cheaper, and in many cases free (e.g., Skype, GoogleTalk, providing they are not banned in your country). A call from Pakistan to the U.S., for example, cost approximately $2 a minute in 1990; now it's about two cents. This means more business communication costs are lower.

Sending email is free. Compare that to the cost of a stamp to send a letter from Oman to Jordan. Now everyone can access any market from where they are. No barriers exist.

Education in America was superior to that of many other countries. The "brain drain" occurred as the brightest and most talented in the world were recruited by Harvard, Yale, and Stanford. Thousands of other universities gave their graduates a head start in life because they had the smartest professors. Now, teachers and thought leaders have their own blogs and websites and give presentations at events that are captured on camera and uploaded to YouTube. You do not have to physically attend the greatest universities to get the knowledge you want access to. Professors can build on each other's knowledge online from where they are, rather than having to emigrate.

We also can learn from negatives of the U.S. economy. There is a constant need to get more in American culture. More marketing, for instance, means a new computer game or must-have gadget comes out every few months. The constant need for new products creates wealth but sometimes at the expense of other aspects of life.

In a society that is too money-driven, family time shrinks, because it does not produce as much wealth as office time. We have to be sure to measure other meaningful assets. A home-cooked meal, for example, takes longer, costs less and generates less wealth than a meal at McDonald's. Drinking tap water does not produce as much wealth as Coca-Cola. But they are healthier, which is important in the long term. Your country probably doesn't want to follow America's example when it comes to health: Remember, 30% of its population is overweight.

Emotional wealth is important, too. Even if you have a big number in your bank account, if you are unhealthy you won't be able to enjoy it. A New York investment banker might earn more than a street vendor in Damascus, but he is also likely to have less time to himself.

11. INTERNETOLOGY: THE IMPACT OF THE INTERNET ON LIFE

Think about how much time you spend at your computer. For many of you it is more time than you spend with your family. You probably spend more time at your computer than you do eating, walking, drinking or reading.

In this chapter we discuss how the Internet has impacted society. It may be worth discussing these points with your colleagues as you might realize the Internet is not just another tool you should take for granted.

Education

Education is one of the most important elements of a society. Humans pass on knowledge so future generations can progress. Education can apply to everything from mathematics and history to religion and sports.

There is inequality in education, too. If you are born into a rich family, you could afford to attend a university. This would lead to a better job and a better income.

The most important aspect in education is the quality of teachers. It is not the buildings or any of the other facilities. If the teacher is good, the student will learn. If you grew up in a village, there was not much choice when it came to teachers. Teachers might have used out-of-date methods such as rote learning, in which children just repeat what the teacher says. You wouldn't have learned to think critically. Many teachers in the village who taught English, for instance, didn't speak the language very well themselves.

If only we could "scale" great teachers? The Internet allows us to do just that. Visit www.KhanAcademy.org for thousands of free lectures from Sal Khan. YouTube is full of millions of demonstrations, from "how to kick a football" and "how to become a better presenter" to "how to lose weight" or "how to use Microsoft Excel." Video is not the only medium for Webucation. Bloggers such as SethGodin.com, Entrepreneurs- journey.com, ProBlogger.com or AmirAnzur.com provide regular free knowledge. These websites have become a way of teaching the world.

Teaching used to be a relatively low-paid profession. Your creativity was limited because you had to cover the school board's curriculum to a set number of students, maybe 30. You would have to repeat the same lessons year after year. The Internet brings natural competition. Great teachers will get more visits to their website from links. They can monetize their lessons, too, either from advertising or by charging a premium for selected content.

Knowledge used to be restricted. You had to go to an Oxford or a Harvard to be associated with the best professors. The universities had all the textbooks. Now they are available on Amazon. Even $800 ($20 per book x 40 books a year) is a lot cheaper than university tuition. Most knowledge is already free. Wikipedia replaced the encyclopedia, which used to cost a few hundred dollars, and Wikipedia is more up-to-date, has more content and is free.

A few decades ago, teachers could stay ahead of their students with the teachers' edition, which had all the answers. Now students can get ahead of their teachers by going online. Teachers should not see this as a threat; in the Internet economy, it will be difficult for teachers to stay ahead. Anyone with enough time can look up almost any topic and become an expert within a few days. Students can read ahead by researching on the Internet. The role of the teacher will be more of a facilitator than a person who has all the answers.

Teaching methods will change as well. Traditionally, students would get taught at school and then go home and do their homework. Now students can learn at home through videos on websites such as KhanAcademy.org, Lynda.com, udemy.com, or WebpreneurAcademy.com, then go to the classroom to discuss their problems. Peers will help each other learn rather than relying on just the teacher. This method encourages students to communicate with each other, and, because they are involved in the teaching, improves retention.

Adult education will also grow. Adults who were too embarrassed to learn to read properly, for example, can discreetly search online for help. Once adults gain skills they might have missed in their youth, society will be much more productive. With so much new knowledge being created, adults will continuously have to reeducate themselves to keep up to date for their jobs.

Similarly, women whose education was limited in their part of the world will now have the ability to take control of their education and rise to the level they choose.

The digitalization of books allows people to upload audiobooks that they can then listen to on their phones, while driving or walking. Once people get into the habit of listening to knowledge rather than music, the productivity of society will increase.

Teachers and other members of society should be encouraged to share their knowledge, especially in their native language, whether that is Arabic, Bengali, Hindi, Swahili or Urdu. It is a community's responsibility to generate so their youth can help educate themselves. As of November 2011, there were 3.8 million Wikipedia articles in English, 420,000 in Swedish, 160,000 in Arabic, and 100,000 in Hindi. Languages such as Swahili and Urdu have fewer than 25,000.

If you can simply learn English, you have a wealth of knowledge at your fingertips, but you should also concentrate on creating knowledge in your local language. Governments should invest in local-content producers, and teacher and parents should start sharing their wisdom in their own language online. This spreads education to many people for whom it was previously inaccessible. English might be reserved for the upper class in some countries, so there must be a concerted effort to translate as much content as possible.

Wealth is not limited. If you make more money, it does not mean someone else makes less. In fact, it is often the other way around. The more money you make, chances are the more your neighbor will make, too. If more websites go up in Swahili, it means more Swahili speakers go online, giving local entrepreneurs more places to advertise and communicate about their products and services. If no one in your country is online and you have only one TV station and one newspaper, it is difficult to get your message out, especially if you aren't friends with the producer or the editor.

This point is so important that I will repeat it. Wealth is not a zero-sum game. In the traditional economy, we were taught to compete. There could only be one number one in school. There were only a few promotions available in corporate jobs. We learned that if others won, we lost. With wealth creation, if your neighbors have more money, they can spend money on your products or services. You can create more wealth in a rich neighborhood than you can in a poor one. When you feel like you discovered a secret on the Web, if you share it with those around you, they might come back a few days later and teach you an application of that secret. The smarter those around you get, the smarter you will get!

In America there are 13 million millionaires – out of a population of 320 million. This makes 4 % of the country millionaires. The number of millionaires is increasing everyday so you have a bigger and bigger market of the rich able to buy your product and services. America was the richest country in the world and you had no access to it, until the internet came along.

In the world of medicine there is what is known as the placebo effect. Up to 30% of patients can take a placebo (i.e., a tablet that looks like medicine but does not contain any active ingredients) and feel they have been cured. There is a similar effect when a country sends its students to a local top-tier university. The term "diamonds in, diamonds out" means getting into Harvard is just as important as the education you receive there. Students who gain confidence and feel bright then go out and accomplish more in life.

All the knowledge you need to be successful is online, but there is no placebo effect, the "you are special" feeling top universities engender. Just remember that you can and will be successful if you continually invest in your knowledge and have confidence in yourself. If you do not have confidence in yourself, you won't take action or achieve as much as you are capable of. More confidence leads to more action, which leads to more results.

Let's look at how books used to be distributed. In the old economy, if you were a kid in the streets of Somalia you were likely to be at a disadvantage compared to a kid from Upper Manhattan. When the latest computer programming book was released, for instance, parents in New York City could buy it for their child at a local bookstore. By the time the book, which was relatively expensive because of shipping costs, made it to a (probably) second-hand store in Mogadishu, the knowledge was outdated.

With the Kindle, the iPad or other eBook readers, people can access books at the same time. A Kindle costs $70. Current titles run around $10, while those without a copyright — the works of Shakespeare, for example — are free. An eBook reader can hold over 1,000 books and is portable. Governments in emerging countries could strike deals with big publishing houses in the U.S. and Europe to translate and sell native- language copies for a fraction of the English titles to encourage local knowledge while still paying the authors. Parents around the world no longer have to feel like their child cannot get the best education unless they move to the U.S. or Europe.

In the old model, students learned because they had to pass exams. If they didn't pass the exams, they wouldn't progress to the next level in their class and society would look down on them. This is called "education push," as students learned because they had to in order to progress in their classes or were forced by their parents. "Education pull" is when students learn as they are interested in the learning and is much more effective since it leads to more specialization. Remember, the world rewards those who are the best at something, not average at everything. People will pursue their passions and strengths, giving them a better chance at success.

In the push model, people constantly work on their weaknesses.

The push model said that if you had a D in Mathematics and A's in your other classes, you should work on your mathematics more. The pull model, says if you don't enjoy mathematics and are not good at it, focus on your writing or English instead. There is only a limited amount of time in a day and you can try to learn a bit of everything or simply pick a niche or skill in the world and focus on that.

Relationships

The Web is having more and more of an impact on our social lives.

In many Muslim countries, for example, men socially interact with other men, and women with other women. Facebook allows you to "friend" anyone. In many homes women will be allowed to friend only women but this is changing. Borders are also being broken; it's easy for a Brazilian to make friends with an Iraqi.

Facebook has ushered in a new celebrity culture. A few decades ago, we could see the lives of Hollywood and Bollywood stars in magazines such as *Hello!* and *OK!* or TV stations. We knew where Tom Cruise went on vacation and whom Julia Roberts was dating. Now we are all celebrities. Your friends check out your profile and know your relationship status and where you are going on holiday. Gossip-magazine editors used to decide who was worth following and whose pictures to print. Now you can choose whom to follow online.

INTERNETISM

This can add pressure to succeed. Pre-Internet, you might not have kept up with your old school friends. If you gained weight, so what, nobody would know. On the Web, everyone from high school, university and old workplaces knows what your life is like. We must be careful not to succumb to extreme capitalism.

We end up going on holidays just so we can "tag" ourselves looking cool snowboarding in Switzerland. We start obsessing over losing weight so we look good in photos. We get depressed because we measure our success by what others think of us.

We buy more clothes; people have already seen us in that T-shirt. We look into plastic surgery; our friends look so much younger and nose jobs are all the rage in Hollywood. It might be easier to invest in Photoshop and edit out your imperfections from every picture.

Take the time to appreciate who you are, as imperfect as that might be. Inner confidence will get you further in life than perfect teeth, plastic surgery or a handbag will.

We also have more temptations. Just as the Internet is responsible for starting many relationships, it is responsible for breaking up just as many. One in five Americans met their spouse online. In the United Kingdom 42 % of people have tried online dating. A knife can be used to prepare a nice meal — or to stab someone.

Technology isn't good or bad, it cuts both ways. The Internet brings the benefits I mentioned in this book, but you should use it with caution, because it does not always support our values. A drunken picture of you in a bikini might be OK in Dutch culture, but it will be considered inappropriate to a Saudi. It's up to if you want to ignore these differences, but make a conscious decision as it influences the way you are perceived
online and off.

Successful online personalities are authentic. People can sense when you are true to yourself. You don't puff on cigarettes at a party but worry, in the back of your mind, that your parents might see a photo of you and disapprove. Either quit smoking or make sure you are comfortable and honest about your bad habits. Life is a lot easier if you can be yourself.

Some people live secretive lives (you might never see their spouse or children) while others are very open. Decide who you want to be. For instance, you might want to hide your relationship status on Facebook, and use it as a networking tool. Or you might decide not to "friend" any potential work colleagues and use the account for your parents, spouse and close friends.

The Internet connects many different segments. For parents in the East, setting their children up for marriage is a huge responsibility. Through websites such as Shaadi.com, many are finding appropriate partners for their children. There are niche sites helping connect Muslims to Muslims, Sikhs to Sikhs, Jews to Jews and Indians to Indians.

As the world gets even more mobile, you will have opportunities to work in different regions. The Internet will help you feel close to your family, even if you live apart.

Interracial marriage is now considered normal. In the Internet economy, we will see even more international mixing because people won't be limited by geography. A certain segment of the world will seek to do something "different," rather than integrate with their own "tribe" (nationality, religion, etc). This may cause distress, for example, for the parents who hoped their Hindu-Indian daughter would marry a man from the same caste, but who connected instead with a Muslim-Pakistani.

Teenagers are notoriously secretive. Through Facebook, a parent can get to know their children better. Then again, Facebook might become "uncool" if parents follow their children's profiles.

The point is, whatever you share about yourself on the Internet can be seen by your boss, your spouse, your mother and millions of strangers. So use common sense and post only things you feel comfortable with.

Work

Working conditions should also improve in the internet economy. We've talked about jobs that will be created, but the Web should also make redundant low-level jobs such as data entry.

You used to have a bank teller check your account balance. Then you could do so at an ATM. Now you don't have to leave home to check your balance, change your personal information or apply for a loan.

The nature of work will become more **creative**. Management and administration were the skills needed to move up the ladder in the industrial society. The best degree you could have was a Master's of Business Administration.

Most billionaires in the past decade made their money as innovators. Universities should offer Master's of Business Creation instead of MBAs. Businesspeople can no longer just follow a management guide. They need to learn how to create.

More companies are doing more with less. Facebook can handle 1.2 billion users with fewer than 3,000 staff. People will start smaller companies with global networks. You might start your own advertising agency but outsource translation and video production to small companies.

Repetitive types of jobs can be done by computers, which will do them cheaper, faster and better or be outsourced to an emerging country. Borders will not protect jobs anymore.

The line between "I am at the office" and "I am at home" will be smudged. You can have more time with your family, but that time will be interrupted by email and phone calls. You will need to work hard and train yourself to check emails and phone calls when you want, not when other people want you to.

The more globally integrated the supply chain becomes, the more work has to be done 24 hours a day, seven days a week. Sunday might be a day of rest in London, but it is a working day in Saudi Arabia. There is an 11-hour time difference between Los Angeles and Dubai, so business partners in these cities will have to adjust their work hours to accommodate their global partners. The workweek will be less structured.

More women will enter the workforce. Many corporate jobs have "glass ceilings," which prevent women from reaching the top, but the world of small business, with its relatively low startup costs, creative freedom and less-structured hours, will attract talented women who happen to have families.

People will become less robotic at work. We tend to act differently at work, with our friends and with our parents. Online social networks help break down these barriers. People will see a different side of their colleagues, which will help them bond. Family photos or pictures with old school friends show your human side.

Many talented people from developed countries will move to places such as the Philippines and India to hire their startup teams, and why not? Resources go further in an emerging country and you can develop your employees face-to-face, all the while experiencing another culture.

Culture

In the past century, American culture influenced global culture. Jeans and a T-shirt seemed a lot cooler than the traditional Pakistani and Indian "Shalwar Kameez." Coca-Cola and McDonald's became ubiquitous.

This happened in America because the U.S. harnessed the power of TV and cinema. If you see a cowboy smoking a Marlboro cigarette and wearing Levi's jeans in a movie, you want to do it, too. But Hollywood wasn't interested in Arab or African culture.

Musicians from the U.S. also became famous with youth across the world. Companies such as Proctor & Gamble spread their messages to the world. American brands such as Kellogg's, Harvard and Nike came to dominate.

Why was this? America tried out business models before other countries, because there was more competition. The U.S. government was laissez faire when it came to the economy, as demonstrated by its hands- off broadcasting policies. Compare that to Arab countries, where TV frequencies were used to promote government policies, not Cornflakes. American producers created shows, which companies used to advertise their products. As TV and cinema spread to the rest of the world, the U.S. had a head start.

This is happening with the Internet as well. American companies such as Google, Facebook and Amazon are famous around the world. A Webpreneur based in Afghanistan doesn't have a big enough home for his or her innovations. Afghanistan just didn't "get" the Internet in 1999 like Americans "got" the Internet.

Culture will go back to being local again despite globalization. Young filmmakers can spend a few thousand dollars on a video camera and editing software that would have cost millions of dollars a few decades ago. They can also upload it to websites such as YouTube, which becomes their distributor for free. Viewers in emerging world markets will have to discover ways to monetize their content, perhaps by embedding advertising within the movies.

Now local talent can emerge from around the world. YouTube is a democratic way to push talent to the world stage. You can perform a school skit, and the video can be circulated to all the parents in your community. If it is good enough, the local TV station will air it and even international media might become interested. Doubt it? Look at some of the videos on this list of Internet sensations: YouShouldHaveSeenThis.com.

With almost no distribution costs, it is easier for authors, playwrights and poets to publish their work. You do not need access to large markets to promote your ideas. A free website or mobile phone can transmit content to the world.

You can become a community journalist. Mobile phones are one of the best content-creation devices ever created, allowing you to shoot video, record audio, take pictures or type a blog post.

The problems we face as teenagers — body image, braces, acne — will now be more public. Most of us have never taken media training, so be sure to build up confidence so you can handle being famous. Remember from the Simple Wealth Formula: The more people you impact, the more wealth you create, so, like it or not, more people will see your pictures. Get used to seeing yourself.

Religion

Religion is an important part of billions of peoples lives around the world. Religion though is also going to be massively impacted by the internet. On the one hand religion will grow again. With new ways of reaching non-religious people around the world, the internet is used as a recruiting tool. Used to recruit and organize religious people around the world.

On the other hand religions will weaken especially in countries which had dominated their citizens with a single way of believing. If these countries are not good at censorship people will be able to connect and pick out all the inconsistencies in their holy books. They will be able to convince their colleagues about how they have been brainwashed. A growth in non-believers will occur with the likes of Richard Dawkins and Sam Harris able to convey their messages of non-belief to the world.

Extremists will also grow in number. As the internet enables all sorts of people to connect to each other, extremists will also be able to recruit more people just as non-believers will be able to grow their numbers.

More sects within religions will emerge. More people will start more religions as they master the online world of marketing. Just as Scientology, Mormonism and other religions have emerged within the past centuries so will newer religions at an even faster pace.

Governments

The Internet will cause major obstacles for governments. In the old economy, everything was controlled. Governments owned most media outlets and gave licenses only to people they deemed worthy.

Everyone can be a journalist. Citizens, armed with "undercover" cameras — that is, their mobile phones — will break more and more scandals. Politicians and other government officials must be wary of being caught doing anything illegal because news of it will be spread over the Internet. And it won't just be the highest politicians who have to be careful. For the low-level bureaucrats, being broadcast on YouTube will be as bad as being on national TV.

Government needs fewer employees than ever. Most government jobs are tasks performed over and over. These should be taken over by computers or outsourced to a cheaper country. Otherwise citizens are paying higher taxes than they should be paying. The U.K. has already begun to downsize its government sector.

To catch speeders, a police officer used to have to point a radar gun at the car. Then chase after it, pull it over and write out a ticket. The ticket was processed at city hall and mailed to the offending driver, who then had to drive to city hall and pay the fine. Now a camera automatically measures the speed of passing cars and takes photos of those that exceed the limit. An email is sent out informing the driver, who then visits the city's website and pays the fine with his or her credit card. No humans necessary — except to push the gas pedal too far in the first place.

The Internet makes it easier to start protests and movements. The consensus might be in favor of the government, but rebels might be more skilled at promoting their cause. If you believe in something, you can have a much bigger impact now. Let's say you believe more should be spent on animal protection. Start a Facebook group or a website and target politicians or key influencers so they think animal welfare is more pressing than other causes. The more attention your cause gets, the more people will join it.

We used to wait for the right leader to come to power and make the world better. Now every teacher, middle manager and nurse has the power to bring as much change as their president. In the old economy, the media promoted leaders' ideas; now ordinary citizens can start a website and promote their own movement. A teacher can organize fellow teachers and bring change to the school system.

Power in the Internet economy starts with the visitors you draw to your website. The more people who follow you online, the more power you have to make an impact. Celebrities such as Justin Bieber have over 64 million followers on Twitter; that's more than the population of the United Kingdom.

Facebook does not care about what side of the border you are on. Neither do Skype or elance or Google. In the real world, Indians and Pakistanis can not do business with each other, but online Pakistanis can read Indian websites and Indians can order digital content from Pakistanis. They will talk to each other and exchange services; physical borders will not contain them. Israelis can read Palestinian propaganda and Palestinians can watch Israeli propaganda. Areas with fewer political barriers such as Dubai will become even more important as they become intermediaries in disputes.

Governments need to set key performance indicators or dashboards to show to the public how their services such as healthcare, police, education, army etc are performing. These indicators than need to be explained to journalists who then make headlines and stories to show improvement in the public sector.

Collaborations

The Internet makes it easier to collaborate with different people in different parts of the world. Open yourself to the possibility of working with someone from a different part of the world. Even if the venture fails, don't write off the nationality you partnered with.

AmirAnzur.com, Dean, WebpreneurAcademy.com, Chief Simplification Officer, aartec.com

You may not have the money to pay someone a salary, but you can collaborate and share the risk and the reward. A strong and focused Web presence makes it easier to collaborate because prospective partners can check you out. You also don't have to repeatedly explain your goals to every new collaborator.

DOWNSIDES OF THE INTERNET

Intellectual Property

I have written about the benefits of the Web, but what about its downsides? Take this book. It took me many years of research and months of time to put it together. I could have been working with clients instead of writing this book. The money I could have made is our **opportunity cost**.

The first edition of this book took me a lot of time and money, but the next copy will cost me only $1 or $2 to print. If I emailed it, it would cost me nothing. People could copy this book and share it on a file-sharing website. They could change the authors' names, claim to have written this book themselves or print their own advertising inside.

Pirating has had an impact on many business models. Hollywood spends millions to produce a movie in the expectation that people will buy tickets to the cinema or buy DVDs. Studios then invest this money in other movies.

Musicians spend months, sometimes years, writing songs and playing gigs in the hope that people will buy their music so that they can make a living doing what they love.

Authors spend years writing, hoping one day they will recover their sunken costs when people buy their books.

The Internet makes it easy to copy and redistribute. You could copy a book before, but you would still have to pay to photocopy and distribute it. Authors have had to adjust and come up with innovative ways to monetize their products. This book might get copied, but if so I hope it leads to consulting opportunities to compensate for lost sales. Many musicians accept that their music is going to be illegally downloaded, but understand that some of the pirates will become fans and pay for a ticket to a concert.

Most would consider it unethical to walk into a McDonald's, eat a hamburger and walk away without paying. On the Internet, though, many think it's no big deal to watch a movie, read a book or listen to a song without paying. Hamburgers and other goods were the assets of the last century, and intellectual property is the asset of the internet economy. It is just as unethical to copy a digital book as to steal one from a bookstore. Don't forget the real cost was the writing and marketing of the book, not the paper it is printed on.

We all have our own ethics, so I won't tell you what the right thing to do is. If a book is too expensive for you, but you would read it if it were free, should you download it? The answer is up to you.

As you build your business and invest in your ideas, be aware they can easily be taken and improved. The best solution is to be better than everybody else. There are many knock-offs of Apple products, but while the copycats are busy copying, Apple is busy innovating. Once you start building your brand, people will prefer the real thing to imitations. The Internet is aggressively competitive, which is why there is so much innovation online. You must continue to innovate, not just admire what you have already done.

Governments around the world will continue to debate copyright laws to determine whether to live and let live or regulate the Web.

The ethical implications of the Web will be discussed and questions posed: Is it OK to use a Google image for a presentation without crediting the photographer? You might feel it is OK to take an existing idea and improve it, rather than starting from scratch.

My advice is if you want to build a sustainable business, go into an area that is legal, rather than profiting from someone else's work. Not only will you able to sleep better at night, but also you will have a better chance of success in the longer term. You will find illegal activity takes up just as much of your time and wears on you mentally. You might as well spend that time doing something good for the world and keeping a clear conscience.

Protection of intellectual property is important if society is to progress. Imagine spending years building a house, and as soon as it was completed, someone came and took it away. It would be hard to convince you to work on another home.

There will be more protection of intellectual assets in the next decade. There will also be creative solutions to pirating. Perhaps a $100 copy of Microsoft Office will sell for $20 in Hindi, or books will be priced differently in emerging countries so that some money can be recouped.

Cyber Bullying & Defamation

Another downside to the Internet is cyber bullying. Yes, the Web makes it easier for young people to connect, but it also leads to stalking and abuse. People can post defamatory comments that can cause psychological damage, especially to young minds. What can you do? The justice system takes time. In an age when people spend time spreading lies, the best safeguard is to try to avoid making enemies. Tracking down the source of the defamation takes so much time it is unprofitable.

You should be careful when being critical of others or uploading unflattering pictures. We tend not to criticize people in public or share pictures that might make someone uncomfortable. Try to take this attitude online, too. You would appreciate it if it were the other way around.

Journalists knew the consequences of what they wrote about pre-Internet. They could not walk into your home, take a picture and publish it without your permission, or make up facts. There were legal consequences for misinformation and breach of privacy. On the Internet, anyone can write anything. For the moment, there are minimal consequences, although governments are slowly imposing more regulation.

One way to protect yourself, ironically, is to have more online content. That way you control your message, and offer a quick counterpoint to any negative comments.

Online Scams

There are many other scams and fake profiles on the Internet. People can pretend to be someone they are not. The 419 scam, for instance, messaged people about a "dead relative" and asked the recipient for money. We have encountered people looking for investment money, for instance, who Photoshop themselves with presidents to make it seem they are more important. They even claim to have their own private jets, which are really photos of regular airplanes with the scam logo edited in.

You cannot believe everything you read on the Web. The Internet is a great source of information, but also disinformation. This is why building trust is so important. Over time, once you build your brand, people will pay a premium for your services.

Parents must deal with their children's Internet exposure. Many are unaware of "Net nanny" software that blocks their children's access to adult content. Internet education is important not just for the younger generation, many of whom will learn about the Internet in school, but for adults, too.

Dangerous Stunts

There is also the danger that young people perform more stunts to get views on YouTube. For instance, using GoPro cameras or their smartphones to film themselves climbing tall buildings or driving dangerously. The fact that everyone can become a celebrity will cause more people to risk their lives in order to get famous. Sometimes it won't be worth it!

Privacy

The Internet will also limit the privacy an individual has. Governments can use the microphone embedded in your phone to turn on without you knowing as well as follow your every footstep. Through your phone they can know exactly where you are, who you are talking to and what you are saying. This could not only be used by Governments but others that want to spy on you for any reason such as your spouse or boss.

Once you go online your privacy is eroded.

12. WEBONOMICS: BUSINESS MODELS FOR CREATING WEALTH ONLINE

The Internet is a blank canvas. You can paint any picture you want with it. There are thousands of ways to create wealth online, and in this chapter we look at a few of these opportunities.

Marketing

In essence, the Internet is a marketing tool – just like TV, radio, billboards or direct mail. You still need to have a product or a service to sell, but the Internet enables you to attract customers from across the world you might not have had access to.

Business owners want more customers, so if you tell them how you can attract more they are likely to listen.

Take, for instance, a company manufacturing air conditioners. You might propose a deal that for every air conditioner you help sell, you make $100. You would start a website — www.YouAirConditioners.com — market it, then send the manufacturer the orders you get. You get $100 for each sale.

You can also market yourself through YouTube, LinkedIn or even Facebook to get more customers for your services. If you are one of the best graphic designers in the world, for example, you can make money doing it.

Become an expert at Google Adwords or Facebook advertising and promote yourself — from anywhere in the world. Once you learn how to use the Internet as a marketing tool, many companies will pay you for your services.

You can do this on a retainer basis; that is, a company pays you a monthly fee to help it manage its social media and bring in new customers, or by commission, which a company pays you for each new order. The Internet makes it easy to track sales, so it is easier for business owners to pay marketers only for successes.

Online marketing is becoming more and more sophisticated. Lets say that you already know the people you want to target and you have their email address. You can upload those email addresses to facebook and only show advertising to those people. You can create a short advert for those people searching on YouTube for air conditioners. Whereas adverts on television have to be about products or services that appeal to millions of people online they can be targeted at just a handful.

Affiliate Marketing

You do not need to get anyone to hire you to be an affiliate marketer. Many businesses use affiliates to help them sell. You can sign up free to work for a company such as Amazon (affiliate-program.amazon.com).

Here's how this works: Visitors to your website see an ad for Amazon, for instance. When they click, they are directed to Amazon's website. If the viewer buys a book, you get a commission, up to 15% of the sale price. Amazon does not pay you for click-throughs that do not end up in sales. If a customer buys, you win and the company wins.

This method gives you incentive to create a themed website. You could launch BookReviews.com, for example, and offer links to Amazon for every book you review. It will give you an affiliate code, which lets it know the customer came from your website. An affiliate code might look like www.amazon.com/affiliateID=amiranzur. This will tell Amazon when someone clicks through the link where they came from.

What if a customer clicks through to Amazon, but buys the book a week later? Many programs have a "cookie," which is left on the computer of the potential customer. There are 30-day, 90-day and 365-day cookies, so if the consumer purchases the product within the cookie's timeframe, you still get credit for the sale.

Websites such as ClickBank.com offer up to 75% commissions to affiliates. The reason they can offer such high commissions is because the delivery costs of most digital products — eBooks, training courses, etc. — is almost zero. The only cost to them is a 5% credit card charge, so even if a company gives you 75% commission it still makes a 20% profit. Sellers of digital products know they can upsell; that is, offer their customers other products and services in the future. Even if they lose a little on the affiliate sale, they will profit in the future.

Amazon has over 100,000 affiliates. ClickBank.com has paid its affiliates commissions over $2 billion (that's "billion," with a "b"!). Commission Junction (CJ.com) is an affiliate management program that connects you to hundreds of companies that will pay you to help sell their products.

The great thing is that these are free to join and give you a way to start earning without have a product or relationships with any companies. There are affiliate commissions for products and services selling for thousands of dollars that pay out thousands in commission per sale.

You can also join Webpreneur Academy's affiliate program – if you promote the course to your friends or others who might be interested, you make a percentage or the sales.

eCommerce

You can also start online by selling your own products, be they books, DVDs or clothes.

Payment options for your customers can include credit cards or Cash on Delivery. If you sign up with a company such as www.2Checkout.com, it will process credit cards on your behalf, even if you live in countries such as Nigeria, Pakistan, India or the UAE. You can also pay companies such as Aramex to collect cash on your behalf.

PayPal is a popular method of payment in the U.S. but is restricted in many countries. Check its website to see if it is available in your country. To create your online store you can use software such as 1ShoppingCart, InfusionSoft, OSCommerce or Shopify.

Sourcing your product is important. Websites such as www.alibaba.com will connect you to thousands of suppliers around the world that can produce products for you.

You will also need to sort out how to ship your products. FedEx, DHL, Aramex and a host of local couriers can do this for you.

Software

The best way to make money is by solving problems. What can you do to solve an issue and promote your solution? These are some examples of software ideas and companies that have been successful in that field:

- helping people manage their accounting (e.g., Quickbooks)
- helping small business manage their customers (e.g., Salesforce.com, Zoho.com)
- helping people manage their email marketing (e.g., MailChimp, aWeber, iContact, ConstantContact)
- hosting software (e.g., HostGator.com, HostMarkaz.com)
- eCommerce software (e.g., Shopify, ShopMarkaz.com)
- Helping people find their life partner (e.g., Match.com, eharmony.com, shaadi.com)
- Helping people find their closest taxi from their smartphone (Hailo.com)
- Helping people rent out their spare room in their home (AirBnB.com, Couchsurfing.org)

There are thousands of niches (e.g., medical software) in which you can create a computer-based solution to a problem. The more people online, the more who will be looking for software.

Localized software is a growth market. U.S. companies are unlikely to compete with you, and you can already see what worked there. You can customize the software, provide support in your local language and get local newspapers and TV to promote you. If you can create the best software in one country, it should work in many.

The software business model, known as Software As A Service or SAAS, is similar to the one for mobile phones. A customer signs up with a provider, and every month pays a phone bill, let's say $20 a month. If a telecommunications company can get 1,000 customers, it will make $20 x 1,000 = $20,000 per month.

When people sign up for SAAS, they rarely leave, especially if the software does what it is supposed to do. Provide more value than your customer pays for and you will continue to grow your business.

Like Google, you can also give out the software for free and make money through advertising. You might take a loss when only three or four people use your software, but as you start to succeed and attract hundreds of customers, you will see your investment pay off.

When creating software it is important to learn and understand what a database is. A database is at the core the Internet. Amazon is simply a database of customers and suppliers. AirBnB is simply a database of people with rooms to let and people that want rooms to let. A country is simply a database of the passport or ID cards of its citizens. If you can understand databases you will go a long way to understanding the core of your online business.

Education

Another growth sector online is teaching. As people mature, they spend less on cars, watches and handbags and more on self-fulfillment. There are five knowledge niches people pay for:

- Business and make-money
- Health, fitness and weight loss
- Relationships and dating
- Irrational passion
- Formal education

The business and make-money niche is what entrepreneurs like to spend money on. Webpreneur Academy, for example, helps those who want to create a living for themselves. This book also falls into this category.

Health, fitness and weight loss feature products such as acne, abs- building programs and disease cures.
Relationships and dating feature products such as divorce kits and advice for finding the right partner.

Irrational passions feature products that cater to activities such as golf or stamp collecting. Avid golfers will pay for tips on achieving the perfect swing. Formal education features products that help students get into college or degree programs. People pay to improve their GMAT or SAT scores or to get their teaching or MBA degrees online.

Services

There are thousands of jobs you can do online by joining services such as upwork.com, freelancer.com or eLance.com and selling your talent, whether it's translation, graphic design, video editing, software programming, voice- over talent or copywriting.

If you remember the Simple Wealth Formula you know you need to differentiate yourself from the thousands of others selling their services. Some copywriters charge $10,000 for a day of their time, others do it for $5 per hour. Your rate depends on how much your customers are willing to pay. If you do not build your personal brand, employers will simply hire the cheapest workers.

Once you build your brand, the employer can justify paying you $100 an hour since it knows you are the best in your field. To make $100 per hour, you would need to target richer employers and have more valuable skills.

Advertising

Popular websites can integrate with services such as Google AdSense. Over 90% of Google's $30 billion in revenue each year comes from AdWords, the ads on the right side of the page when you do a search. AdSense allows you to integrate those ads into your website and share the revenue with Google.

MyGameReview.com links to Amazon.com in its video-game write- ups. The company makes a commission every time one of its viewers buys the game on Amazon. AdSense automatically inserts advertisements into a website and pays for every click.

Lead Generation

Lead generation is a type of marketing where you could create a website for instance GlobalDentists.com. You could then have people type in their post code or zip code (in the UK and US a post code or zip code tell what area a person lives in). Collect their phone numbers and emails and tell the potential customer they will be called back from the closest dentist.

Each lead can be charged at $10 to $50 or even more depending on what industry you target and how much margins they have. They will pay you as the contact details you provide are of someone that has themselves indicated that they are interested in their service. One Internet entrepreneur I met had spent over $60 million over 7 years on advertising for lead generation of window cleaning businesses in the United States. He would generate the lead, then sell them to various local window cleaning businesses who would call back the potential customer with a quote. They would know they would end up getting one of the three people they called with a quote as customers for hundreds or even thousands of dollars over the lifespan of the customer so were happy to give a few dollars per lead.

YouTube Partnership

You can also make money by partnering with YouTube. You can post a video and if enough people watch it, YouTube will share some of its advertising revenue with you. Every time someone clicks on one of the ads below or to the right of your video, YouTube will pay you a commission.

Ray William Johnson and Nigahiga have over four million YouTube subscribers and make hundreds of thousands of dollars creating videos for YouTube.

Michelle Phan, for instance, records her makeup tutorials and makes more than many doctors. To upload videos onto YouTube is free, and you can post as many as you want. To join the YouTube Partnership program you have to meet certain criteria (visit YouTube.com for further details).

Private Label Rights

Some companies create information products but allow others to sell them. You can purchase the private-label rights to a website-creation tutorial, for example, for a one-off fee of $200. You can rebrand it as your own, then sell it for $50. You would need four customers to break even.

White Label

White label is used to associate products with a successful brand. The larger company offers the use of its brand, but does not participate in production. A hosting company like www.hostgator.com allows you to become a reseller and whitelabel its solution. They allow you to rebrand the solution so that you could call it www.MyHostingCompany.com and instead of charging $5 per month charge $20 per month. You have to generate the customers but keep a major share of the product. Whereas an affiliate program builds someone else's brand while a white label solution builds your own brand. This is how Aamnah (www.aamnah.com) created her hosting company www.HostMarkaz.com.

Trading

In the old economy to trade stocks and shares you would usually have to move to a city such as London or New York. Now you can trade stocks, shares or foreign currency through the Internet with companies such as e-trade.com.

Buying stocks is about being able to look at publicly traded companies such as Apple, IBM, Google and Microsoft and predicting if their share price will go up or down. To be successful, you need to study a decent amount of finance, but it is possible to make a decent income trading on the Web. There are many tools available online that enable you to buy and sell virtual shares, allowing you to get some practice without losing any actual money. You can checkout www.finance.yahoo.com or www.etrade.com for actual trading.

Property

You can buy, sell and rent properties through the Internet. Websites in countries such as the U.S. and the U.K. let you know the price of all neighboring houses and what they sold for. For instance, www.foxtons. co.uk gives you a virtual tour of a property so you can see what it looks like.

Websites such as Zillow.com help you find property prices in different parts of the world. The markets in the U.K. and U.S. are usually more defined and transparent, and with higher rates of foreclosures recently there is an opportunity for you to pick up cheap real estate and buy and sell it without visiting the country. This is why establishing trust is so important; people from another part of the world need to know they can rely on your brand, especially when it comes to something as important as a home.

Drop Shipping

Even if you don't have a product yourself, you can do what is known as drop shipping. You receive an order but direct another company elsewhere in the world to buy your product or service. You have no inventory, which means your costs are low. You just pass on the orders when you get them to the appropriate manufacturer. This would be the equivalent of an Amazon.com store receiving an order for a Sony TV, then letting Sony know to send the TV straight from the factory to the customer.

In the pre-Internet economy, you would have had to buy the actual TV, and if you didn't end up selling it, you would lose out. This way you do not have to invest in inventory. Many people are doing this on websites such as ebay.com and amazon.com. They research items where they can make a profit and advertise them on ebay or amazon.

Venture Capital

Through the internet you can become a venture capitalist especially if you live in a wealthier part of the world. Through geo-arbitrage it means your regular income as an accountant might be $3,000 per month. You could take 10% of that income and invest it with an entrepreneur in an emerging part of the world to develop an idea that can go global. This would have been difficult before the internet came along as if you lived in a richer part of the world, you would have needed to finance an entrepreneur from your part of the world and you might not have been able to afford those levels of investment.

You might meet a smart student from a university, for instance, and decide to partner with him or her. You pay the base salary and they do the research and put the business together.

If you get the right people on board, you can eventually build up a good-sized company. Investing in your own business is much more exciting and potentially financially rewarding than putting money into a bank account. Just remember, venture capitalists must be prepared to lose all their money if the idea doesn't work out — and many ideas don't work out. Try to establish your own affordable loss, or an amount you can afford to lose.

You might have a day job that gives you a decent, stable income, but there is an inner entrepreneur inside you. Team up with someone you can afford to hire from a different country and have him or her experiment with your money. While you receive the steady income from your job, your business partner in a different part of the world experiments to help you both make a much bigger income.

Websites such as CrowdCube.com allow you to raise money for your company or to invest in others looking to invest.

Consulting

Probably the cheapest way to get started is through consulting. Look in magazines and newspapers for companies paying a lot for advertising – these will be the ones paying for full-page ads. Check to see if they have an online presence. If not, go ahead and start offering your services. You can price out each part of the service you offer such as Google Adwords management, facebook fan page management, website build, Search Engine Optimization etc...

13. THE QUICK-START GUIDE TO BECOMING A WEBPRENEUR

If you want to create wealth in the Internet economy, there are three main aspects you must master:

1. **Mindset** – You will face many people who tell you it can't be done. You will have many moments of doubt. You have to stay positive throughout your Webpreneurship journey. If it were easy, everyone would do it. Without the right mindset, even if you do succeed, you will not enjoy it.

2. **Business Knowledge** – Some people think the Internet is some magical machine that spits out money. The business world will always be competitive. You will not make money out of thin air; you still need to provide value. Traditional skills such as marketing, public relations, people management and finance are still important.

3. **Internet Skills** – Your Internet skills are the final component in making a living in the internet economy. Define your goals and understand that the Internet is just a tool to help you achieve them. When you to decide to go from Abu Dhabi to Dubai, a car is just the method of transportation. Without a destination, you would just drive around in circles. Use the Internet to build your education or career; that is, get to your destination.

We have developed a wealth-building program at the Webpreneur Academy and are working with educational institutions such as GEMS and Repton to integrate it into their curriculums. Here is an overview:

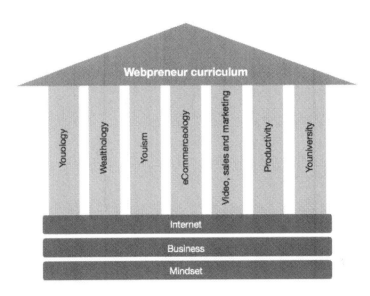

YOUOLOGY: KNOW YOURSELF

"Everybody is a genius. But, if you judge a fish by its ability to climb a tree, it will spend its whole life believing that it is stupid."

– Albert Einstein

The first step in creating wealth is knowing yourself. If you do not have clear goals, you will not know what direction to go. Draw what is known as a career window. This box helps you to gain perspective on your long- term future.

You are in window A today. Ultimately you want to get to D. Often it is not possible for you to jump from A to D in one step. First you might need to go to B, then C before reaching D.

Let me use my own career window as an example. While at university, I decided I wanted to be an entrepreneur but didn't think I knew enough about business to start my own. So I crafted a career path from student to entrepreneur:

Accenture	Microsoft, Virgin Media, Oracle, Boots Retail
University	Txfo.com

I joined a management consulting firm (Accenture) straight out of university to gain experience. This allowed me to work with clients such as Microsoft, Virgin Media, Oracle and Boots Retail. I gained the necessary confidence and experience to eventually start my own technology company (Txtfo.com).

A few years after setting up my business, I decided I didn't feel my work had fulfillment and meaning like I wanted. I thought being my own boss would bring me happiness, but it didn't. I stress how important it is to know yourself first, because it will help you get into the right field. A business can take many years to establish, so you might as well be doing something that gives you meaning and fulfillment.

I decided meaning would come from helping others create wealth, especially in emerging countries such as Pakistan, where he I was originally from. I had to craft another career window, this one from running my own business in London to helping others in emerging countries.

I sold my business, got an MBA and moved to the UAE. I worked at the Knowledge and Human Development Authority, then at the Abu Dhabi Education Council. I learned about education in a country that brought together some of the best teachers in the world, but still got paid. Eventually, I started what came to be known as the Webpreneur Academy.

From entrepreneur to entrepreneur with meaning:

IMD MBA, Switzerland	Knowledge and Human Development Authority, Government of Dubai, Abu Dhabi Education Council, UAE, Ministry of Education, Pakistan
Txtfo, United Kingdom	Webpreneur Academy, United Kingdom and Global

Notice how I didn't make the transition in one step. It took years to go from rain to sunshine, from an entrepreneur to a student to an employee to an educator.

I maintained my networks from different parts of the world, rather than starting fresh every time I changed base. I might physically have moved from London to Lausanne to Dubai, but my Facebook/ YouTube/LinkedIn friends knew as much about what I was doing as they did about their friends at home. I knew from his career window that I would eventually need these people to help him to reach his goals.

If you are working in sales and marketing for a telecoms company in Kuwait but dream of being a Hollywood actor someday than go chase your dream. Perhaps first get a job in sales and marketing for a telecoms company in Los Angeles. Then get a job in sales and marketing for a movie studio. And from there make your connections to get your big break. Staying where you are and simply dreaming will not make it happen.

The Internet can help you get into almost any industry. You might love football but realize your dream of turning professional is not realistic. But you can start a fan website, interview players on Skype, sell football shirts online or design a football video game. The point is, if you love doing something, it won't feel like work. To win in the Internet economy, you have to put in the time to become the best at what you do; there isn't a lot of easy money.

In the book *Outliers: The Story of Success*, Malcolm Gladwell says it takes 10,000 hours to become an overnight success. I worked many long hours for years before achieving any moderate success. Mark Zuckerberg might seem to be an overnight success, but he had a one-on-one programming coach in his teenage years, long before he invented Facebook. Bill Gates started programming when he 13, many years before he founded Microsoft. Focus on your long-term goals because the journey will be a long one.

You might as well enjoy the scenery along the way, so remember to study Youology. The Internet allows you to do what YOU want. To create success in your way. If you don't have passion for what you are doing and just follow the script set by your parents, teachers or boss, your chances of success are lower.

Mark Zuckerberg did not create Facebook so he could make a few million dollars, sell his company and retire on a beach; he has a passion for connecting the world. Steve Jobs did not turn up at work each day so he could increase returns for his shareholders. He was crazy enough to think he could change the world. Bill Gates did not run Microsoft because he wanted the power. At a time when computers were enormous wall-sized contraptions, he had a mission to put a computer in every home; Microsoft has not achieved this but is getting closer. Successful people find their DNA and pursue what is right for them.

WEALTHOLOGY: KNOW THE GAME

You can't win a game unless you understand the rules. The earlier chapters should have familiarized you with how wealth is created. Remember the simple formula for creating wealth:

	Amount of Value You Can Add
X	Number of People You Can Impact
−	Number of People Who Can Do What You Do
−	Cost to Serve
=	Total Wealth Created

All you have to do is simply figure out a way to add value to the world.

The more education and skills you accumulate, the more value you can add. If you know how to touch type, for instance, you can produce content faster.

Figure out ways to impact more people. How can you scale your business? The billionaires of the world have impacted millions. How can you create something that can impact more people?

Adam Smith wrote about specialization. How can you get into a field that few others are in? In the world of medicine, for instance, specialists (such as neurologists) typically earn more than general practitioners. How can you brand yourself so that you are known as the go-to person in your industry?

How can you reduce the cost to serve? Will you pass the savings on to your customers or increase your profit margin and use that money to continue innovating? Perhaps you can hire people in different parts of the world who specialize. The better your personal brand, the more people trust you, enabling you to get down to business faster. You would be more likely to invest in a venture if Bill Gates approached you than a stranger.

YOUISM: SPREAD YOUR IDEAS

"Be yourself, everyone else is already taken."

- Oscar Wilde, author and playwright

Once you've studied yourself and determined your career goals, you are ready to brand. The Simple Wealth Formula posits that the better your brand is, the fewer people who are perceived to be able to do what you do.

You must be aware of everything that affects your brand. The university you attended, for example, could impact your brand as could your country. Online products that are Made in Nigeria, for example, are harder to sell than Made in California. Don't let this stop you; there are benefits to being where you're from. You can also give the image that you are based in New York, London or Dubai without having to live there.

Imagine we met for a few minutes at an event. If we don't connect through a social network, it will be difficult for us to see what interests we have in common.

On Facebook, however, you could see what friends we have in common. On LinkedIn, you could see companies we worked for.

Use online social media tools to build connections, even though it might be years before you do business together. We have people we haven't seen since high school approach us with business opportunities. But since they trusted us then, they are willing to do business with us now.

Wealth in the Internet economy is not simply about money. Your connections are a great asset. Someone with a million followers on Twitter has a resource that could potentially be worth more than a million dollars. If key tastemakers such as Barack Obama, Oprah Winfrey, Nelson Mandela, Mark Zuckerberg, Larry Page (Google) or Sheikh Mohammed (Ruler of Dubai) read your blog, you have the potential to create a great deal of wealth and influence the world.

It used to be difficult to reach CEOs or top politicians. In the Internet economy, you can reach any kingpin of society online with effective marketing. Your opinions matter more than at any other point in history.

You can produce blog posts (articles), YouTube videos or podcasts (audio programs) to build your following. The more fishing poles you have in the water, the more fish you are likely to catch. Similarly, the more content you produce, the more followers you are likely to attract, especially if your content is high-quality. Content is your new fishing pole.

To get started with www.YourName.com as your own domain and website, go to www.HostGator.com. Get a domain and use the open source Content Management Software such as WordPress, Joomla or OpenCart to start your own website.

ECOMMERCE: DO BUSINESS ONLINE

"Every one lives by selling something."

- *Robert Louis Stevenson, author and poet*

In order to make money, you have to actually sell something. You could be an affiliate marketer (e.g., Amazon) who helps others sell things, or you can sell your own products and services.

Students who have studied at the WebpreneurAcademy have ended up selling honey (SabeelHoney.com), skin-care products (MedColl.ie) and freelancing (aamnah.com). These entrepreneurs all had a passion to export something to their part of the world or to import something.

What is your passion? Do you know of any products you want to import or export? You can put up your own website on sites such as ShopMarkaz. com that enable you to get your own domain such as MyOwnShop.com rather than using other people's domain. Remember one of the assets you are building is value of your domain brand over time.

Price the products how you want. You can accept Cash on Delivery (check Aramex.com), PayPal or credit card (check 2Checkout.com or alertpay.com).

Let's imagine you are based in Nigeria and want to target American consumers. Unfortunately, Nigeria doesn't have the best reputation on the Web with Americans. Pakistanis, Libyans and Yemenis will have similar issues. But you can register a company in the U.S. (for about $600) and make the whole operation seem like it is based in New York. You can visit a website such as Grasshopper.com to get a U.S.-based telephone number that forwards to your mobile or to Skype. You can get a U.S.-based address through companies such as ShopAndShip.com and have your mail forwarded. You will have to file taxes, but the whole set- up costs about $1,000 and should take just a week to set up.

You can also register companies in the UAE through sites such as www.vz.ae. The cost, $10,000 a year, is more expensive than in the U.S., but having a Dubai number and visa might be worth it for people from Afghanistan, Iran, Iraq or Pakistan, which do not have strong global brands. The benefit is also less regulation than the US or Europe and no taxes.

eCommerce will continue to grow as more and more people realize the convenience of shopping via the Web or mobiles. There might be fewer Web-savvy consumers in your part of the world, but there are also fewer competitors. If you focus on being a big fish in a small sea, you will have an advantage when the rest of the world moves into your local market.

VIDEO, SALES AND MARKETING: TELL THE WORLD

"Half the money I spend is wasted; the trouble is I don't know which half."

- John Wannamaker, Retailer

Once you have something to sell, you need to tell the world about it. No one will buy from you unless he or she knows about what you have to offer.

In the traditional economy, companies spent millions advertising in newspapers and magazines and on TV and radio and billboards. The problem was no one knew what their return on investment was. Were a million people watching a TV program or were there only 100,000? How many walked out of the room once the commercial began?

Was it worth paying $10,000 for a half-page ad on page 3 of Time magazine or on the back cover of Newsweek? It was expensive and hard to target. Amateur advertisers found it hard to get into the game. It wasn't worth the risk for a mom-and-pop shop to make a TV ad because the owners didn't know how many would watch it. It was difficult to start small. But you can start advertising on the Internet with a few dollars, and scale when you know what works. You can measure exactly how many consumers looked at your ad, how many clicked through and in which country they are based.

You can define different ads for different markets and continually test and improve them. Once you spent a few thousand dollars putting up a billboard at the side of a highway, it's difficult to change if it isn't working.

You can create high-definition videos to spread your word using a relatively inexpensive video camera or mobile phone. ScreenFlow and Camtasia Studio offer screen-capture software you can use to record a PowerPoint presentation. You can use voice-over if you are uncomfortable in front of the camera, or hire professional voice talent from sites such as upwork.com or voices.com if you don't like the sound of your voice. Now you have a digital product to sell. You can promote it by doing guest posts on other people's blogs or having famous (i.e., well-followed) online personalities interview you. You can use your social media profiles on Facebook and Twitter to sell; remember, if you promote yourself too much, people get annoyed. Think of subtler ways to add value; write a blog post about how to promote a book to attract more followers. Google makes most of its money in advertising. If you do a search on Google, you will see businesses have paid for their ads to appear on the top and right sides of a page.

The advertisers bid for keywords. For instance, a handbag company might offer $1 to Google Adwords for every time someone clicks through to a website after the search: "buy handbags online." If someone bid $1.10 per click, his or her ad would be seen above yours, making it more likely to be clicked on.

In the traditional economy, there was a local phone book that listed phone numbers for plumbers, electricians and hotels. In the Internet economy, more and more people search online for these products and services. You can target your customers more precisely. Someone who types "buy handbags online" is not looking for a plumber, otherwise they would have typed "local plumbers."

The great advantage of the Internet is that it is so measurable. This is where your high school mathematics comes in. If you sell handbags for $60 and your cost to make them is $20, your profit is $40 per sale. For every 10 visitors who visit your website after searching for "buy handbag online," one ends up buying.

You can afford to spend $40/10 visitors = $4 per visitor to visit your site. If you spent $3 per click, you would spend $30 on Google advertising to attract 10 visitors with one of them buying; you would make $40 - $30 = $10 profit. If you spent twice as much you would likely make twice as much profit.

If only one in 100 end up as buyers you can spend $40/100 visitors = $0.40 per visitor. You should bid less than 40 cents for each visit. There is a lot of math involved, but it's not too complicated.

There are two tricks to selling online. First, you need to improve the conversion rate of your website. You want more than one buyer for every 10 visits.

Of course, you also want more people to visit; that is, to increase your traffic. Instead of 100 people visiting per day, how can you make it 1,000? The other way to reach the top of a search on Google is what is known as doing Search Engine Optimization. These are natural search results you do not need to pay Google for. There is an art to this, but basically Google wants to give its users the best experience possible. The company tends to give weight to the number of links to a website.

Wikipedia, for example, is at the top of many search results because many other websites point toward the online encyclopedia as the authority on a subject. The more websites that link to your site, the more authority Google thinks you have. If important websites such as CNN.com or BBC.co.uk link to you, you have even more importance.

Facebook also gets a lot of traffic, and uses the pay-per-click method, too. Unlike Google, however, Facebook does not use keyword searches to determine its advertising. Instead, it sells advertising based on a user's "likes." On Google, someone might use the search "buy Arsenal shirts," for instance, whereas on Facebook he or she might have joined the group "Arsenal Football Club."

Facebook also allows you to target according to age, gender, country, education and even workplace. A job posting might read: "Women, aged 25 to 35, living in Jordan, with a university degree who work at HSBC bank." The more tuned in to your target customer, the more effective your ad and website can be.

Compare the effectiveness of Google and Facebook to traditional TV, radio and newspapers. If you were to advertise pet food, for instance, on a major TV channel you would pay tens of thousands of dollars for a 30-second segment. Your ad on pet food would be broadcast to millions of viewers, many of whom would not even own a pet. A small percentage of viewers would buy your pet food, (if they remembered it the next time they went shopping).

But when you advertise on Google or Facebook, you already know something about the consumer, either from a Google search or a Facebook profile. You pay only for people who are interested enough in your product or service to click through and visit your website. More and more people use credit cards to buy online, so the transaction is often immediate; that is, the consumer won't forget.

You can target a niche anywhere in the world online. Maybe you know that women in Saudi Arabia like a special type of Brazilian skin oil. An online Mexican beauty website can target Saudi women and sell them a Brazilian product.

That said, you are still more likely to do business with your neighbors down the street than someone a few thousand miles away.

PRODUCTIVITY: BE EFFECTIVE

If you were asked to dig a hole, would you use a shovel or a teaspoon? If you are paid a high hourly wage, there is no incentive to work faster, so you would use the teaspoon. The longer you take, the more money you make.

Bureaucrats often use teaspoons. They get the same salary at the end of the month and if they do their paperwork more effectively, their reward is more paperwork. Effective bureaucrats are either motivated internally or by public recognition.

Entrepreneurs are rewarded for output. They are usually paid by the hole rather than for how long they dig. They would use a shovel, or a digging machine, if they can find one. Entrepreneurs try to do as much as they can in as little time as possible.

Many people do not take the time to improve themselves. They keep doing things the slow way. You should try to be faster online. Learn to touch type, for instance, as it is more efficient than the "hunt and peck" method. If you double your words per minute, you cut your typing time in half.

Remember, your time is valuable, so you want to save it as much as possible. PCs crash more, have lower battery lives and are much slower to use than Macs. Faster Internet connections would also significantly increase your online productivity. If you are always forgetting your passwords, try LastPass.com, a free tool to help you keep track. Want to share big files across many computers? Try dropbox.com. Use sites such as Upwork.com when you don't understand how to do something online. You can fiddle around for hours trying to put your website up, or you can save time and hassle by hiring someone for $7 an hour to do it for you.

Be ruthless with your online time. Do not get stuck in endless chats or Skype conversations. Just because you are not paying a telecommunications company for the call does not mean it is free: time is money. Nothing breaks the workflow like a phone call, an instant message or email. Shut these things off when you are working and you will improve your productivity drastically.

So, you want to become a millionaire? There are eight hours in a regular working day, 40 per week. If you work 48 out of 52 weeks a year, your total working hours would total 1,920.

$1,000,000 / 1,920 = 520 per hour.

You need to generate $520 per hour to make a million dollars in a year. Education (reading this book), and networking can help, but watching cute kittens on YouTube or chatting about the latest celebrity gossip will not.

This is an age of multitasking, but focusing on a single job at a time is much more effective. Try this exercise. Have two of your friends take a piece of paper and draw out three columns. In the first column write down odd numbers (1, 3, 5, 7, 9); in the second, write out the months (January, February, March, April...); in the third, write down even numbers (2, 4, 6, 8, 10).

So the finished page would look like this:

1	January	2
3	February	4
5	March	6
7	April	8
9	May	10
11	June	12

Have one friend work across the columns ("1 January 2," "3 February 4," "5 March 6, etc."). Have the other write down the columns ("1, 3, 5, 7, etc.,") then "January, February, March, etc.," then "2, 4, 6, 8, etc.".

You will notice people doing the single-focused task (i.e., the second way) are able to complete their tasks quicker than those whose brain has to think of an odd number, a month, then an even number. When your brain can focus on one thing at a time, you are a lot more efficient.

In a world that is more and more filled with interruptions and has more and more choices, it is important to be able to focus on your own goals. Do one task at a time. As an entrepreneur you will sometimes feel overwhelmed with all that you can do and should be doing. Focus on the task at hand and do it well.

People often ask if they can start a business when they are still at university or working. You can, but you will have to sacrifice the time you spend watching TV or gossiping with your friends. You will have to be efficient with your time after class or work so you can work on your business. You might even have to sleep a little less.

Watching football or discussing politics with people who have no intention of being in the game won't add much value to the world. Starting a website can have an impact. If you've studied Youology and understand your own goals and dreams, you will want to be more productive. You won't want to waste hours watching endless videos on YouTube.

Productivity is an endless cycle. You have to continually look at your methods and how you can improve them.

YOUNIVERSITY: LEARN TO LEARN

More and more ideas are entering society through communication. Printing a book was a big deal a hundred years ago and relatively expensive after the invention of the printing press, but the Internet has made it free to produce and share knowledge.

The way to win in the knowledge economy is to become the best in your niche or industry. In order to become the best, you have to keep track of the latest trends. You must be efficient in the way you consume knowledge.

Let's say you spend half an hour each day commuting to and from work. Most people listen to the news on the radio or music. The problem with news is you can't really control the stock market crash in New York or the war in Iraq. It's a shame if there is an earthquake in Bolivia, but you can't do anything about it. What you can control is what happens inside your circle of influence.

The one hour a day you spend commuting to and from work adds up to five hours a week or 20 hours a month. This is 240 hours a year. This works out at 240 / 8 = 30 full days (i.e, six full weeks) that you could be learning if you were listening to audiobooks. Instead of having to read, listening to an educational book on the way to and from work over a year is the equivalent of six weeks of learning in a university every year. How much more knowledge will that mean for you, especially over your lifetime as you have simply made effective learning time from what you were using to listen to the news or music? Wouldn't that give you a better chance of success in the knowledge economy?

Turning your car into a university is a great way to enhance your knowledge and we strongly encourage you to fill up your mobile phone or car CD player with audiobooks so that you can educate yourself while commuting.

And you no longer have to pay for a lot of university education. You can visit iTunes University and get over 350,000 free lectures from professors at Harvard, Oxford, Stanford and the London School of Economics.

A few hundred years ago, if you did not go to the right university you would not get the right job. Universities had libraries with hundreds of thousands of books. Now anybody can access those books.

Teachers now market themselves by giving away their knowledge via blogs. For instance, visit www.amiranzur.com and you can access plenty of free information. We give out valuable content to show our worth, then make money from seminars and speaking engagements.

You don't have to monetize knowledge, either. Many share what they know for free, to better the world. You can no longer blame your lack of knowledge on your economic station. All of us — governments, corporations and citizens — should help others gain access to the Internet and teach our children to learn to learn.

You have an important tool after you understand the Internet's wealth- creating possibilities. Plumbers can take online courses to become better plumbers. They can also learn to do their own books with online accounting tutorials.

You are not limited to local knowledge. A plumber from Bolivia can learn about best German plumbing practices. You could become the magic plumber of your village by importing these techniques. You can then raise your fees since you are not in direct competition with less- knowledgeable plumbers anymore. They might copy your secrets, but you will be constantly coming up with new ones since you are plugged in to the online international plumbing community.

This is how you truly create wealth. Be the best at what you do. Bring value to the world. The key to being the best is knowledge. Why learn by trial and error on your own, when you could save yourself years of work by learning from someone else?

There was a study to measure what species were able to travel one mile using the least energy. The condor, a type of bird, was at the top and humans were a third of the way down the list. Not at all the most efficient of the Earth's creatures. But then someone compared the condor to the human on a bicycle and humans were far the most efficient of all the species. We have the knowledge and tools to win almost any game!

As humans we continue to improve the way we do things. The Internet can connect you to anyone across the world to gain knowledge, and that is its true power.

14. YELLOW SHIRTS VS. RED SHIRTS

Try this simple experiment. Take a group of people from your school or organization and randomly divide them into two groups. Give one group yellow shirts to wear for a few weeks and the other red shirts.

Now watch how communities begin to form. The yellow shirts might start saying things such as: "The red shirts are so arrogant. They never start conversations with us."

Then the red shirts will chime in: "The yellow shirts are not as smart as us. We do all the work. They just copy us."

Even though the teams were chosen randomly, opinions are formed based solely on the color of people's shirts.

This is what the world has become.

We have been randomly divided into countries and religions, professions and skin color. These brands give us a sense of identity.

In the U.K., grown men get into fights over football teams. Is it really worth it to punch someone because he supports Arsenal and you are a Chelsea fan?

In other parts of the world, the fights are over religion or borders that were drawn up long before any of us were born.

Do not judge 300 million Americans because of their president. A leader of the country, whether it's George W. Bush or Barack Obama, does not represent the entire population. In democratic countries, at least 30% of voters support the losing candidate; that is, three out of 10 people do not agree with their country's strategic direction. Presidents and prime ministers get more media coverage, but this will change in the Internet age. Now, any one of the "red" or "yellow" shirts can represent their brands.

A country also should not be judged because a few terrorists did something horrible. Or a race judged because a few commit crime. Or women judged on the clothes they wear, whether it's a burqa or a mini-skirt.

People have the right to live their life with their own culture. The Internet enables us to connect with many types of "weird" people, but don't impose your view of the world on them; appreciate them for who they are. If you want to influence the world, be a good person yourself; others will choose to follow you if you set a good example. Do not go to other parts of the world and try to force people into seeing that your view of the world is right. Once you begin to appreciate different viewpoints, you can begin to appreciate commonalities, too.

Brandism exists and many people will judge you on your religion, nationality or weight; that is, qualities you cannot control. If you want to create true wealth, do not judge people on their brand. If you are Pakistani and do not like working with Indians, you are throwing away a billion potential customers, all because of a line on a map drawn up by bureaucrats decades ago. You might think it doesn't matter what you think about your customers; it is just business, after all, right? The truth is that it shows. It comes out in your work or art.

If you love what you are doing and whom you are doing it with, you will pay attention to the details that matter. If you lack the desire to deal with your clients, the care will not be there and the quality of your product or service will suffer.

In the Internet economy, those who find ways to work with people from different cultures are more likely to be successful. Remember, wealth is created when people exchange different skills. Go to places where you are unique rather than surrounded by your own clones!

END PASSPORTISM

The world is now made up of close to 200 countries. A century ago, it was completely different. In 50 years, who knows what the borders will be?

European borders have disappeared over the past few decades, while in Sudan new dividing lines have been drawn. The world keeps shifting, as humans keep erecting artificial barriers and differentiating their brands (i.e., countries).

The Internet allows us to live in a world in which we are not judged by the color of our shirt, where a Filipino can make more than an American and a Kenyan bank is more trusted than a Swiss one, where people, products and services will be judged by their quality rather than their stereotype.

In the 1950s, branding was done by skin color in the U.S. Black people were not able to get the jobs white people could. They could not travel. Martin Luther King Jr. had a dream that one day his black children would be able to play with white children and that people would be judged by the content of their character rather than the color of their skin.

The idea of a black president or an African-American TV mogul seemed impossible back then, but in 2008, Barack Obama was elected and Oprah Winfrey hosted the most-popular TV show. Blacks now hold prominent positions in every field, from politics and entertainment to science and literature.

It might be hard to imagine a person from a lower socioeconomic class in your country holding a prominent position, but it will happen. A Brazilian living in Australia might have as much of a chance to lead Germany as a Berliner.

A world without brandism might not be too far away. The Facebook and YouTube generation don't fear unknown brands like our parents did, even if some people still promote distrust. A good place to begin this breaking down of barriers is through sports. It's important to appreciate these contests for what they are: branding exercises. Support your country if you like, but note, too, how each country has its own logo (flags) and theme tune (national anthem).

Remember to always be a positive ambassador for your brand, whether it's your school, workplace, city, country, religion, skin color, gender or even disability. Ultimately you will make it easier or more difficult for the next person from your team to find work. Make sure that whatever shirt you end up wearing benefits.

15. FINAL WORDS FOR THE JEAN-PIERRES AND IMRANS OF THE WORLD

Wealth is created when ideas, products and services are exchanged. Automobiles, trains, phones, newspapers, radio and TV brought great wealth for people in the last century as they allowed us to connect and trade with each other. This century will bring even more wealth as the barriers to entry on the Internet are much lower, meaning even more people will have access to create wealth.

The Internet is a tool that gives us the ability to access two billion people regardless of their geography. This number will grow significantly for the next five billion as smart phones and 3g and 4g networks bring the internet to even more people.

The biggest barrier to entry to the Internet is education. Unless someone shows you exactly what is possible, you won't know what you don't know. Many will miss out on the greatest wealth generation tool in the past 1,000 years. We need to let others see the possibilities of the Internet and how it can be used to greatly improve education society's wellbeing.

Remember the Simple Wealth Formula:

	Amount of Value You Can Add
X	Number of People You Can Impact
–	Number of People Who Can Do What You Do
–	Cost to Serve
=	Total Wealth Created

Figure out yourself how the Internet can help you with each of the factors. Even if you do not use the Internet, you can still manipulate the factors to generate more wealth.

The Internet brings down barriers so the Imrans of the world have the chance to compete with the Jean-Pierres. Passports and other barriers governments put into place do not prevent people from competing anywhere in the world.

The U.S. was a country that created a tremendous amount of wealth in the past century, mainly because of its investment in infrastructure such as roads, railways and TV. Companies such as Nike faced criticism when they opened shoe factories in countries such as Vietnam when workers in the U.S. were unemployed. But remember, the other workers in the U.S. were taking care of a different part of the value chain, creating advertising for local markets and being the face of Nike (e.g., Tiger Woods, Michael Jordan).

Jobs did not disappear, but were spread throughout the world. The Internet is causing the same thing to happen. Your French teacher might actually be based in France; your website might have content written in England, hosted in Germany, and designed in Kenya with products sourced from Japan.

Many Americans complained about how China was taking away its jobs. Companies such as Apple now count China as their second-biggest market and see huge growth there. If you are competitive and ready to fight, then the new economy will create a tremendous amount of wealth for you. If you do not like competing and want to keep the wealth your family obtained through government connections, then the Internet will not so great for you. It will foster transparency, making it easier to detect corruption.

You need to figure out how to deliver value to as many people as possible. You have no excuse of being in the wrong country or not having the right education.

The Internet will help developing countries emerge, and lift millions of people out of poverty faster than at any time in history. To create wealth we need knowledge, and to spread knowledge, there has never been a greater tool than the Internet. A hundred years ago, one teacher could impact a few hundred students. You would have to move to a university in a different part of the world to learn about the latest thinking. Now professors are able to visit your home virtually and teach you at your convenience in any part of the world, many of them for free.

It has never been a better time for the poor to get richer. In the farming economy, you needed to own land in order to be truly wealthy. The most likely way that you could grow your wealth was through inheriting land from your parents, which allowed you to buy even more land and grow your wealth further. If you never inherited land, then it was hard to climb up society. In the industrial economy, the way to get richer was to own a factory. To own land or a factory, you needed a lot of capital in the first place. So chances were if you were born into a poor family, you couldn't afford to get on the ladder to create more wealth.

In the Internet economy, the assets have become ideas and the ability to execute on those ideas. You do not need to buy land or have the capital to set up a factory. A great idea and perseverance will help you create wealth and get to the top of the wealth creation in your society. You do not even need to have money to go to the best schools because if you invest in yourself, you can help yourself get the best education and network to be able to win in this economy.

You need to invest in your knowledge, skills, tools, brand and network so that your ability to execute great ideas becomes better and better.

In the Internet economy, we can do more with less. Through my websites www.AmirAnzur.com and www.WebpreneurAcademy.com I can reach millions of people; only two decades ago that kind of reach would have required hundreds of employees and business relationships. You, too, can start your own website and start teaching the world.

The Internet also connects you to people across the world who can help you bring change to your local village, whether by buying or selling products and services or exchanging ideas.

Do not look at the Internet economy as a short-term investment, which, if it doesn't work out in a few weeks, it wasn't meant to be. Look at it for the next decade of your life and beyond. Is the Internet going to be an even bigger part of people's lives? Decide for yourself, and, if you are convinced, spend as much time as you can (an hour a day? an hour a week?) discovering how the Internet will work for you. It will take hard work, patience and some trial and error to determine business models and sustainable methods.

LESSONS IN ENTREPRENEURSHIP FROM THE CHINESE BAMBOO TREE

The Chinese bamboo tree has to be watered and fertilized everyday for 5 years and hardly grows in its first 5 years of its existence. If in those 5 years the tree is not watered or fertilized it will die in the ground. In the 5th year though it grows 90 feet in just 6 weeks.

The question is that does it grow 90 feet in 5 years or 6 weeks? The answer of course is 5 years. That's how long it took to grow it. To build the foundation. To get the people. To build the network. To learn the market. To nurture it. To learn the system. To learn how to do it. To figure it out.

Entrepreneurship and chasing dreams is also often like the Chinese bamboo tree. Nothing seems to be working. Nothing on the surface seems to be growing. But you must have faith. Faith that consistent action towards your goals will lead to the eventual growth of your tree.

Remember that few people seem to appreciate the Chinese Bamboo Tree while it is in the ground laying the foundations. Some people will come make fun of the farmer that puts so many years of work without much to show for it on the surface. They will tell the farmer to pick another crop, which shows the results much quicker. But the trick is to be the farmer with faith. Faith that your hard work and perseverance will eventually pay off. To ignore the voices of doubt that come when a few months or years into your farming you ask yourself "will it ever grow?". To keep going and know that putting in the work, will lead to the eventual growth of your tree.

To be a successful Chinese Bamboo Tree farmer you need patience, consistent action and faith that your tree will eventually blossom too.

In the internet life, we often only notice the 6 weeks of growth of other people's trees, but we often don't truly appreciate the 5 years of watering and fertilization farmers have done on the road to success.

If your tree hasn't blossomed yet, have faith, patience and keep going with consistent action until it does.

BE YOURSELF

Oscar Wilde said: "Be yourself; everyone else is already taken." What worked for me might not work for you, and what works for you might not work for anyone else. We each have our own DNA, and you have to find yours.

Wealth in the Internet economy is not just about the number you have in your bank account or the car you have in the driveway or the number of rooms you have in your home. These material things are less important as measures of wealth.

Instead: How many views do you have on your YouTube channel? How many followers do you have on Twitter? What unique skills do you have? What languages can you speak? Who is reading your blog? Who can you influence? Who trusts you enough to collaborate or recommend you? And ultimately are you content with what you have and where you are heading? These are the new currencies of wealth.

Ultimately, you might not want any of the above. You might be content where you are. That is the ultimate goal, not to win the game by earning the most money but finding fulfillment. Only you can discover how. Remember, the Internet also enables us to lead the lifestyle we desire. You might choose a business model, in the short term, that fits the way you want to live. Longer term, you will be successful once you love what you do.

My hope is that this book inspires you to take your journey on the Internet to the next level. I hope you now have the confidence that there is a future online for you. You do not need a computer science degree, just a passion to do what you do best and the desire to be the best in the world at it. Use this amazing tool to help your ideas go global or simply dominate the local market.

Unless you jump into the water, it is difficult to learn to swim. Reading is great, but jumping in the pool is what will turn you into a swimmer. Unless you do something with the knowledge you just read, do not expect to have wealth come to you automatically. You must take action and provide value to the world in order for you to get richer.

The Internet has leveled the playing field. The question is: Will you take part in the game or simply watch from the sidelines?

16. AMIRISM: THE STORY OF A WEBPRENEUR

"On the internet anybody can make up a quote and I think Amir Anzur is a genius."

- Nelson Mandela

Remember that there are no barriers to giving advice so when gaining any new knowledge you might wish to first ask who is the source. I would like to begin this book with a little introduction of the teacher so you can see the importance and the credibility of the book to have an impact on the world as well as why it was written.

There is a group of people born in America known as the ABCDs - American Born Confused Desis. Desi referred to as the term for people originating from the subcontinent (Bangladesh, India, Nepal, Pakistan). These were the ones who are confused of their belonging with mixed thoughts about whether they belong to the East like their parents or to the West like their friends in school. I am not an ABCD but am however a BBCD. British Born Confused Desi.

Born in the United Kingdom to parents of Pakistani origin I have often asked myself philosophical questions of identity and culture. Am I from the West or the East? Should I live in Europe, America, Middle East or Pakistan? Why do Americans and Europeans earn an average of $45,000 per year while people from the subcontinent earn less than $2,000 per year?

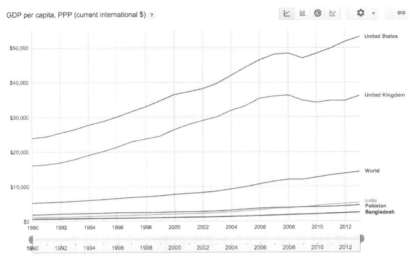

GDP per capita, PPP (current international $) ?

A difference of wealth. What an average citizen earns per year - Source: World Bank

Why does terrorism happen? This question particularly after the tragedy of September 11th, 2001 sent me on a quest. I had a choice to either be ashamed and continue reading about the "bad guys" from my part of the world or to do something about it.

By 2006, the constant reading and watching terrorists originating from the Muslim part of the world and often from Pakistan made me decide that I was going to do something about it and figure out why all this happens and how it could stop so we have a safer and healthier world.

You can look at the past 8 years of my life as a PhD research paper – except instead of writing my thesis so that a handful of academics read it, I have written this book with the hope that as many people as possible read it and benefit from it. I have put things in as simple format as possible so that teenagers and adults around the world understand the concepts and the power of the Internet.

Yes – the title of the book is "Internetism: How to Create Wealth in the Internet Economy" and I concluded that the Internet is the great opportunity that the world has to head towards a direction that we want it to go towards. And if you are reading this book than I am assuming you want a safer world without bombings and wars. And you also want a wealthier world where you have better health care, needs of the poor taken care of and more money for you and your loved ones to spend as you please.

This sounds like an idealist but not a realistic book. But I promise if you stick with me until the end of the book and give yourself a chance to discuss some of these points in your class or your office, you will see that the world will be a better place after all. I'm not promising that all this will happen overnight but if we work as a team than the world can get much better, much faster.

My own Internet journey began in 1999. I was working in London for Accenture, the world's largest technology consulting firm. I was 22 years old and was already bored of the corporate life. Was this it for another 43 years of my life I thought? I was tired of the long hours working for someone else. I wanted to start my own business of some sort. I kept looking around but you needed money to start most businesses and although I was getting paid well I didn't have enough to buy a restaurant or start most types of traditional businesses.

In 1999 there was a big hype about the dot-com boom in the United States. There were stories of people making millions online and this attracted me. I had a degree in Computer Science that I had completed in 1998 and although I had come across the Internet, I didn't really pay attention to it during my studies. Reading about the dot com millionaires though got my attention.

I started investigating what the Internet was all about and suddenly I could see that the Internet was going to change the world. In 1999 there was no YouTube, no facebook, no Google Maps, no AirBnB, no Wikipedia, no Uber, no KhanAcademy, no Coursera, no Smartphones with Internet access everywhere.

From the moment I truly understood the Internet I believed in it enough to leave my high paying full time job to pursue my ventures on the Internet. I saw back in 1999 that the Internet was going to change the world not only in Silicon Valley, but in London and Islamabad as well. As you will read later on in this book different parts of the world change at different speeds.

I didn't know exactly what I was going to do but with so much opportunity I thought I would figure it out. I left London as there weren't too many people that understood the power of the Internet around me. I eventually got an apartment in Las Vegas and started working on my ventures. Armed with a credit card, lots of passion and the confidence that I was good with computers – I had graduated top of

my class at the University of Manchester and won computing awards in my school –
I was sure I was going to make it.

Within a year though I had run out of cash. I was broke. I couldn't get any
further credit. Desperate, I went back to Accenture and begged for my job back.
Accenture kindly agreed to take me back. The next few years I was depressed and
living through the embarrassment of being a business failure. They say that
entrepreneurs go through many failures before they become successful but I didn't
know that at the time. All I knew is that I had told my work colleagues and friends
that I was going to be rich online and now I was back at work with a huge amount of
credit card debt to pay back.

By 2003, I had cleared my credit card debts and got my lucky break. Due to the
tougher economic conditions I was offered a redundancy package. I could take
$70,000 to leave Accenture or else take a pay-cut by moving to another department.
This was what I needed and I took the money.

This time I was much smarter with my cash flow. I would conserve cash. I
bought tons of books and started reading heavily. I went to technology fairs to
understand where the world was going.

I saw that SMS text messaging on mobile phones was a big opportunity and built
apps around it. I started a company from scratch having to come up with the name,
brand, figuring out the business model. I would end up with txtfo.com, taking it
from just an idea and zero revenue to $250,000 in revenue.'

I didn't make millions through the web but made enough to make a living online.
In 2007, I got an offer for the company and sold it to a larger industry player.

Running txtfo taught me about being an internet entrepreneur. That it would
take experimentation and a lot of pivoting until the idea clicked. That I would have
to learn about traditional business skills such as Sales, Marketing and PR as well as
the online skills such as web development and online marketing. And that a
business was a business, if you could make one business work you could start
another product or service and make it work.

Having sold the company I could now think of what I wanted to do next. I built
up several online businesses including a flowershop, hosting company and
insurance. I started getting asked more and more questions from friends on how to
start their online businesses.

I was living in Dubai at this stage and saw that there was a serious lack of internet literacy. People used websites such as facebook, Google, YouTube and LinkedIn but no one had really taught them how these websites. I constantly got asked how do I make money online.

So I started teaching it. I founded Webpreneur Academy (Web + entrepreneur). I taught people in rich countries like Roz Martin who went on to sell several million through her business selling beauty products online. Women like Soraya Chiah who would leave her job in Insurance to sell services for tourism online. People like Aamnah who would earn $1,400 – what an average Pakistani earns in a year – in a month from her bedroom in Lahore, Pakistan. Women like Dr. Sarah who would sell over $25,000 of honey online. And women like Fatima Paruk who went from never having owned a website to generating over $150,000 online selling cake baking supplies online.

I took on a variety of students. Some from Western countries like the United States, Ireland and Moldova and many from developing countries such as Bangladesh, Kenya and Pakistan. This in turn taught me a lot more about the Internet as after I showed students the basics they would often come back to me to teach me how they had started earning online.

For me, the past 15 years have been like watching things happen in slow motion. I've had ideas that someone finally invented many years later. And I learned the hard way that it wasn't only about the innovation but also getting heard too. That this book will go and compete with millions of other books on the virtual bookshelves. My websites would compete with hundreds of millions of other websites on the web. My voice will compete with billions of other voices in the world.

The Internet is simply a connection tool. It has allowed me to somehow connect to you. My hope is that you will be as optimistic about the world turning into a better place for all of us. I was lucky to be born in one of the best-run countries in the world, the United Kingdom, where healthcare and education are free and yet still regarded as amongst the best in the world. I also had the privilege of coming from one of the poorest countries in the world, Pakistan, and so am able to write a book that explains the impact of the Internet in the poorest parts of the world as well as the richer parts of the world.

Many of the poorest countries never got to see the benefit of computers over the past three decades. Computers were simply too expensive and providing electricity to run them was also a challenge in developing countries. Now though shopkeepers in a poor part of the world can do their inventory management through an Android based mobile phone that can keep power even as the electricity goes out for a few hours. There is less and less differentiation between a $60 mobile phone as apposed to a $600 mobile phone. They both connect to the Internet but the price point means that the poor of the world can start competing globally too.

It has become easier for countries to catchup. My time in London means that I can order my groceries through tesco.com and choose the 30-minute slot that they will get delivered at right to my home. I can order my taxi on a phone app like uber.com which locates all the available taxis which are closest to me and gives me the estimate of the price and time for it to come pick me up. When I go on holiday I can rent out my room on www.airbnb.com and someone will pay me to stay at my place. I can make an income online through selling my knowledge at WebpreneurAcademy.com.

The level of education and disposable income will differentiate how someone in a rich developed country like the United Kingdom or the United States will use the internet as opposed to someone in Pakistan or India. However, there will be a general trend towards which the world will head.

In my best month I've made USD 50,000 through selling software online. I didn't invent Google or Facebook but am one of millions of people that managed to earn a decent income through the Internet. Over the past decade I have met countless millionaires who lived the internet dream. People like Russell Buckley who sold his company AdMob to Google for $750 million. Or Paul X. who has spent over $70 million on Google Adwords – imagine how much he has made.

Since 2009, I have been teaching others about how to earn an income through the internet. I taught firstly informally and then formally through another startup of mine, WebpreneurAcademy.com. In this time I have seen some of my students create million dollar businesses whilst others have managed to leave their day jobs to earn a decent income online. I have taught rich people living in Dubai and taught poor people living in Pakistan. I've taught students from over 40 countries.

I was an idealist. The internet could help everyone I thought. But I realized that it has its limitations. This book is part autobiography, part cultural, part economics and part about the internet. I realized that the internet is not one thing for everybody but there are many different implications for the internet including on people that will never use it.

The World Is Not Really Flat

One of the first questions I get asked is how long will it take me to start earning. The answer is that it greatly depends on who you are and where you are currently. Some people within a few months start earning. Some take a few years. Others never make it. It is also not appropriate for everyone to earn online as many are happier in non-technology based jobs.

Bill Gates had access to a computer at the age of 13 before most adults had even seen one. Mark Zuckerberg had private one on one coding lessons which his father paid for. It isn't blind luck which makes people successful online but advantages given by parents that have a significant input.

I hope you find this a useful book and if so I would appreciate it if you could forward it to your friends. If you have any comments or suggestions just send me an email (amir@amiranzur.com).

The pioneers are the ones who have the arrows on their backs. I am a pioneer of the Internet and have had many years of bruising and doing things the hard way over the past 15 years of experience. The internet is here for another 15 years and this book will help you make the most of those 15 years.

So who is this book for? Firstly it is aimed at the corporate employee who is either looking to get ahead in her career or perhaps to even step outside the corporate world to start her own business like I did. It is also aimed at the students that are looking to gain the best skills to be ready for the Internet economy or earn while they study. And finally it is aimed at Governments many of whom have employed me over the past few years to help advice them how they can build a better society for their citizens.

I have failed online more than anyone I know. At one point I had over 300 domain names with 295 of them not making any money. That is a lot of experimentation. I have spent countless hours thinking, reading about, discussing and analyzing the internet. I have paid tens of thousands of dollars learning from internet gurus. This is a culmination of years of research simplified.

17. HOW TO MAKE MONEY THROUGH THIS BOOK

So how can you actually make money through this book? My aim is to actually help you create wealth.

1. Use this knowledge to know that it is possible and to help you continue and accelerate your journey online. Believe in the internet and believe that it is not as difficult as it may seem. It is becoming easier everyday to become a Webpreneur.

2. Give this book to someone else and if they end up buying any of the products or services that I offer and let me know they heard about me through you I will give you 10 % of whatever I earn from them for a year. Currently, for instance I am selling Personal Strategy Consulting for GBP 5,000 (+VAT) per month. The commission would be GBP 500 per month. If they stay for 12 months you make GBP 6,000.

3. Go to Internetism.org and download the co-author version of this book. The book has been written so it looks like two people wrote it. You and I. It basically has the same things as this version of the book but is less personalized towards me.

You can add, delete or change any of the text so you really do become my co-author. You can then go to www.CreateSpace.com - a company owned by Amazon.com – which will allow you to upload the new book.

AmirAnzur.com, Dean, WebpreneurAcademy.com, Chief Simplification Officer, aartec.com

Take everything in this book and look for "Amir" and replace with your name. E.g. where it says Amirism and your name is James, than make it Jamesism. If it says www.AmirAnzur.com and you are www.JamesSmith.com than replace it. People will think you are an author and this will improve your marketing. You can then go to www.CreateSpace.com and upload the book so it appears on Amazon and order single copies and give out to people. There is also the option to coauthor with me.

ABOUT THE AUTHOR

Amir Anzur is an Internet entrepreneur who teaches individuals and organizations about the Internet, entrepreneurship, innovation and living a good life in the Internet economy.

He won the 2005 European Prize for Innovation and his clients include Amazon, Google, Intel, Oracle, Xbox and Samsung. He is the Dean of WebpreneurAcademy.com, Chief Simplification Officer at aartec.com and author of Internetism.org.

Amir has an MBA with Distinction in Leadership from IMD Business School in Lausanne, Switzerland; a first-class honors in Computer Science with Business and Management from the University of Manchester, U.K.; and an International Baccalaureate from the International School of Brussels, Belgium.

You can learn more or subscribe to his blog at www.AmirAnzur.com.

www.facebook.com/amiranzur
www.twitter.com/amiranzur
www.linkedin.com/in/amiranzur
www.youtube.com/amiranzur

Printed in Poland
by Amazon Fulfillment
Poland Sp. z o.o., Wrocław

82637728R00080